PRIESTS
GNOSTICS
& MAGICIANS

European Roots of
Esoteric Independent Catholicism

By Siobhán Houston

the apocryphile press
BERKELEY, CA
www.apocryphile.org

apocryphile press
BERKELEY, CA

Apocryphile Press
1700 Shattuck Ave #81
Berkeley, CA 94709
www.apocryphile.org

ISBN: 1-933993-68-5

Table of Contents

Dedication

To the Most Reverend Martha Thérèsa Shultz
Requiesat in Pace

Acknowledgements

I would like to express my gratitude to the following people for making this book possible: Dr. John P. Plummer, Dr. Nicholas Goodrick-Clarke, Paul Bialek, Dr. Harry Costin, Phillip Garver (Tau Vincent II), Dr. Gloria Houston, Dr. John Mabry, Tau Malachi, Dr. Graeme Standen, Most Reverend Alexis Tancibok, and Dr. Joel Zimbelman. Special thanks to the staff members at the British Library, the Theosophical Society of London Library, and the University of Colorado at Boulder.

Introduction

As a member of the Independent Catholic clergy and a long-time student of the history of religion, I saw a need for a volume that explores the European roots of American independent esoteric sacramental churches (IESC). While various books, such as Peter Anson's *Bishops at Large*,[1] offer much scholarship about this topic, a broader historical context is often absent. For example, it is useful to understand the complicated relationship between the Roman Catholic church and the secular government of France in the nineteenth and early twentieth centuries when discussing the development of the French Gnostic churches of that era. Similarly, a basic knowledge of Anglo-Catholicism and the Oxford movement is valuable when considering the origins of the Liberal Catholic Church.

Given the highly fluid nature of independent esoteric sacramental churches, it is difficult to create a typology in which to view them historically. John P. Plummer has coined the useful term "independent sacramental movement" (ISM), which encompasses groups having "small communities and/or solitary clergy; experimentation in theology and liturgy; mostly unpaid clergy; ordination available to a large percentage of the membership; a sacramental and eucharistic spirituality, with a mediatory priesthood, in most cases preserving the historical episcopate." These communities are called "independent" because they are autocephalous ("self-headed," i.e., not in submission to any other bishop or church) and not in communion with the mainstream churches of their lineage. As Plummer remarks, "The independent sacramental movement presents significant barriers to academic study. It is widely scattered, anarchic, and sometimes difficult to locate.... In addition, both clergy and laity move with relative ease from one jurisdiction to another."[2]

While mindful of the constantly shifting, overlapping, and interpenetrating nature of ISM lineages and groups, I have created a general classification of the ISM and Independent Catholicism in particular in hopes of assisting the reader to move through this book more easily. I have divided the ISM into four groups: Independent Catholics, Independent Orthodox, Independent Anglicans, and churches founded by prophetic vision, such as Jules Doinel's Gnostic church (discussed in Chapter Two). The first three groups listed share the appellation "independent"; that is to say these churches are not in communion with the mainstream churches in their lineage, although they maintain varying degrees of the originating church's doctrine and praxis.[3] From the category of Independent Catholic come three more subdivisions, which rarely interact with each other and are often at loggerheads:

1) Old Catholics, which I define as those churches who self-identify as "Old Catholic" and that hold to traditional Christian tenets as defined in the ecumenical councils. These churches, in the main, are conservative in liturgy and social teachings, and usually confine priestly ordination to men, although they allow their priests to be married. Under this rubric fall communities like the Catholic Apostolic National Church, the Old Catholic Communion in North America, and the Polish National Catholic Church;[4]

2) Liberal Independent Catholics are generally characterized by loosely interpreted doctrines or theological stances that encompass a wide spectrum of understanding as well as inclusive and liberal stances on social issues. These groups commonly (although not always) ordain women, married men, and gay and lesbian people. Out of this category arise two more subcategories: the esoteric metaphysically oriented churches like the Liberal Catholic Church and Ecclesia Gnostica as well as the Roman Catholic reform groups such Spiritus Christi in Rochester, New York, and Light of Christ Ecumenical Catholic Community in Longmont, Colorado;[5]

3) Archconservative Independent Catholic groups and churches (including the Society of St. Pius V and the Society of St. Pius X), who reject the implementations of the Second Vatican Council and hold to pre-conciliar Roman Catholic doctrine, praxis, and canon law. [6]

This book is geared primarily toward members of Independent Catholic churches with an esoteric and liberal orientation, especially those studying for orders. Since I assume that the majority of readers possess a certain breadth of knowledge about esotericism and related topics, such as the ancient Christian gnostics, the Theosophical Society, and theurgy,[7] I have not gone into great detail on these subjects. I do, however, point readers who would like more information on these and other topics to resources that I have found to be both reputable and helpful.

The study is organized into three chapters, roughly delineated by geographic area. The first chapter examines the origins of the Old Catholic Churches of Europe, beginning in eighteenth-century The Netherlands. In the second, French influences on the development of Independent Catholicism are explored, including the seminal figures of Dominique Varlet, Joseph René Vilatte, and Jules Doinel. The third and final chapter begins with the saga of Arthur Harris Mathew in Victorian Britain and goes on to document the birth and early years of the Liberal Catholic Church. The study ends with a brief indication of the influence of the Liberal Catholic Church in the United States; however, the scope of this work necessarily limits a detailed history of independent esoteric Catholic churches in the twentieth and twenty-first centuries. Plummer's excellent book, *The Many Paths of Independent Sacramental Movement* (Berkeley: Apocryphile Press, 2006), addresses that subject. As the number of scholars researching Independent Catholicism increases, it is my hope that many more published works on this greatly-neglected topic within the history of Christianity will soon be available.

Siobhán Houston
24 June 2009

Chapter One
The Origin and Development of the Old Catholic Church from Seventeenth-century Jansenism to the Early Twentieth Century

Part One: Apostolic Succession in Independent Esoteric Sacramental Churches

The office of bishop is at the crux of any sacramental church, whether it be Roman Catholic, Anglican, Orthodox, or one of the many independent sacramental churches. In particular, whether a given bishop is part of a "valid" apostolic succession is of paramount concern in regard to church identity. A standard Roman Catholic definition of apostolic succession is, "The uninterrupted succession of lawfully-ordained bishops extending from the Apostles down to the present bishops of the Church, who thus have received the powers of ordaining, ruling, and teaching bestowed on the Apostles by Christ."[1] Independent Esoteric Sacramental Churches (IESC) for the most part accept this historically grounded definition, although they may disagree with Rome on what constitutes lawful consecration.[2]

Disagreements over apostolic succession have dogged the Church from time immemorial; Christians have haggled over the question of invalid or irregular clergy for centuries, beginning in the second century and encompassing the fourth-century Donatist controversy to the formation of the Church of England and beyond. This complex and confusing debate becomes particularly heated in independent sacramental churches because of the decentralized and highly fluid nature of the churches. There is no one central independent sacramental authority to adjudicate any disputes along this line.

While there is much diversity between among IESC members in regard to the value of the historic espiscopate, there is a general conviction that, as Plummer notes, "a mediatory priesthood is an important part of a properly constituted Christian Church."[3] For example, Jordan Stratford, an Independent Catholic priest ordained in the Johannite Apostolic Church, put forth this opinion about apostolic succession: "...[E]ssentially I'm convinced that stepping into a stream that was flowing before your great grandparents were born, and will flow once your great grandchildren have died, is ennobling and humbling. A cycle of initiated initiators keeps the work from being about anyone's ego. It invites caretaking rather than imposition. Personally I do not automatically assume the historicity of Apostolic Succession going back to the first century as there's no primary evidence—it seems more likely that the Apostles are masks worn by pre-Christian mystery schools, each with their own 'take' on the lessons of the Jesus Cycle. So AS [apostolic succession] is ultimately a myth, but a pragmatically transformative one."[4]

Since the Roman Catholic Church, due to its ancient

and authoritative presence, is often seen as the apostolic authority by which an independent sacramental church (ISC) must measure itself, a number of these churches focus on authenticating their orders in terms of the Roman Catholic definitions of validity, if not regularity.[5] In the past, independent sacramental churches went to great lengths to document their connections to the apostolic succession in their publications. In recent times, however, this emphasis on authenticating ISC orders in terms of the historical apostolic succession is waning. Many independent esoteric sacramentalists, while recognizing the relative importance of the succession, consider an overly developed preoccupation with apostolic lineages a waste of time, especially those efforts to justify validity in terms of the Roman Catholic Church. They contend that such energies would be more profitably invested in ministry, theological reflection, and collegial work between Independent Catholic communities.

Part Two: The Jansenist Controversy

The vast majority of contemporary American IESC bishops and priests belong to either the line of succession emanating from the French prelate, Joseph René Vilatte, or the British bishop, Arnold Mathew Harris, or, in many cases, both lineages. Vilatte was the first independent Catholic bishop in the United States and ministered in the midwest and Canada from 1884 until 1922, when he retired to France. Although Mathew carried out his ministry in Britain, he is central to American IESC history primarily because of his connection to James Wedgwood, the first presiding bishop of the Liberal Catholic Church.

Over the past seventy years, the lineages of Vilatte and

Mathew have intermingled to such an extent that they are often referred to as one: The Vilatte-Mathew Succession. The ecclesial histories of Vilatte and Mathew are discussed in chapters two and three, respectively. However, both men were ordained in the non-Roman Dutch Catholic Church—Vilatte to the priesthood and Mathew to the episcopate. Exploring the roots of the Old Catholic movement is important to an understanding of independent sacramentalism in the United States. To trace the origins we must travel back to the Netherlands in the seventeenth century and the inception of the Dutch autocephalous Catholic Church.

This chapter seeks to explain the schism between the Dutch Catholics and Rome as well as the the theological contentions of the Jansenists and other mystical currents of that time. Over a century after the official formation of the independent Dutch Catholic church in 1724, these Dutch Catholics supported and eventually allied with the newly-formed Old Catholic movement in Germany, Switzerland, and Austria. Doctrines promulgated at Vatican I (1865-1870) sparked this organization of dissenters, who included numerous leading German-speaking Catholic intellectuals including Johann Frederick Shulte and Johann Joseph Ignaz von Döllinger.

During the seventeenth century, disputes inflamed much of Europe as Reformation and Counter-Reformation forces jockeyed for religious, political, and economic power. One of the most notable clashes, the Jansenist controversy, began in France and revolved around the theological definition of grace. Much larger religious and political issues, including Ultramontanism,[6] Gallicanism,[7] and Enlightenment philosophy eventually attached themselves to this polemic. By the early eighteenth century, the Jansenist struggle precipitated a major clash between Rome and the Dutch Catholics, leading to Rome's break with the Dutch Catholics and the establishment of the non-Roman Dutch Catholic Church in 1724.

The Dutch Catholics did not confess the Jansenists' specific religious convictions, which will be examined later in the chapter. Despite this, the Dutch Catholics were undergoing great tribulations as a religious minority in a Protestant country and could sympathize with the Jansenists' plight beneath the merciless persecution of the Jesuits. In due time, the Dutch Catholics' act of sheltering and protecting the Jansenists caused a conflagration between the Dutch Catholics and the Holy See.

Protestants outnumbered Catholics in the Dutch Republic by the end of the sixteenth century. However, as historian Simon Schama asserts in his monumental treatment of Dutch history, "For in many, if not most, important respects, it is misleading to assume that the Dutch Republic and orthodox Calvinism were interchangeable." Although Calvinism was the "official, and the privileged, denomination," it never became the established church. Over a period of decades, the number of the Dutch republic's confessing Calvinists fluctuated between 10% and 55% of the total population. This left many people who were either members of other Protestant groups or who were Roman Catholics.[8]

The name of Cornelius Jansen (1585-1638), a Flemish Roman Catholic theologian, became attached to the theological debate, although in reality he had little to do with what became known as "Jansenism."[9] Jansen was born in the Spanish Netherlands,[10] studied in Utrecht, and became professor of theology at the College de Sainte-Pulchérie at the University of Louvain.[11] As a young man, he sought entrance into the Jesuit order but was refused. Some speculate that this incident contributed to his subsequent theological quarrels with and general antipathy towards the order.[12] In 1636, Jansen was consecrated as bishop of Ypres. He died two years later of the plague.

The actual founder of the Jansenist movement was a close friend of Jansen, Jean de Vergier de Hauranne (1581-1643), often called St. Cyran, since he was the Abbé de St. Cyran. Both Jansen and Hauranne were followers of Augustinian theology; Jansen's book, *Augustinus*, was published posthumously in 1640.[13] The Jesuit order created the term "Jansenist" to describe the followers of St. Cyran, charging that they advocated the heretical predestinarian theology propounded in *Augustinus*. The Jansenists, also known as the Port-Royalists, rejected both the Jesuits' appellation and their characterization. They argued that Jansen was no heretic, inspired no religious movement, and most importantly, did not propound the heterodox views ascribed to him. Furthermore, they contended that this chimera of "Jansenism" was a convenient vehicle by which the order could attack those who opposed them theologically. Doyle remarks that, "Illusion or not, it [Jansenism] was powerful enough to induce both ecclesiastical and lay authorities in France to persecute those they identified as Jansenist and the institution recognized as their spiritual headquarters, the female monastery of Port-Royal."[14]

The head of this convent during the Jansenist period was Mère Angélique Jacqueline Arnauld (1591-1661). She was born into the celebrated Arnauld family[15] and entered the religious life as a Benedictine novice at the age of eight. Sister of the famous Catholic theologian, Antoine Arnauld (1560-1619), Mère Angélique was appointed abbess of the female Benedictine monastery of Port-Royal while still in her teens. Under the direction of her mentor, St. Francis de Sales, she instituted reforms in the community, including enclosure for the nuns. The Church appointed St. Cyran as the convent's spiritual director in 1636, and consequently the community became the locus of the Jansenist controversy.[16]

Although the town of Port-Royal (located about seventeen miles from Paris) had been the convent's home since 1204, Mère Angélique moved the community to Paris in 1626 because the current buildings could not house all the new members that St. Cyran and his philosophy attracted. Even so, the colony's rapid growth necessitated the establishment of a rural annex, *Port-Royal des Champs* (Port-Royal of the Fields) in addition to the Parisian base.

Under St. Cyran's leadership, the Port-Royal community adopted an excessively strict interpretation of Catholic practice. In addition to contesting the Jesuit teachings on grace, which will be discussed later in this chapter, St. Cyran held that the Port-Royalists were the sole group practicing authentic Catholicism. He believed that a Catholic should withdraw as far as possible from mundane affairs and the world in general. An advocate of a more interior spirituality, he felt that the Church laid too much emphasis on externalities and at the same time encouraged parishoners to regard the sacraments too lightly. Ascetic and scrupulous in the extreme, his followers feared partaking of the Eucharist in an unworthy state and therefore seldom communicated. For the same reason, the Port-Royalist priests rarely offered Mass.[17]

Positive elements of St. Cyran's philosophy encouraged his disciples to read the Bible in the vernacular, engage in small group Bible study, and found *petites écoles*. At these progressive schools, teachers instructed the young students in French, as opposed to the Jesuit and university tradition of teaching in Latin. "In teaching they adopted an openly Cartesian and rationalistic method; they strove to cultivate the intellect and the reasoning faculty much more than the memory, and they appealed constantly to personal reflection." This effective style of pedagogy, which emphasized cooperation over competition and sought to create a warm, supportive ambiance in the classroom, impressed the French and gained much good will for the Port-Royalists.[18]

The movement also drew together well-known French intellectuals, including Blaise Pascal, Antoine Arnauld, and the playwright Jean Racine. John McManners rhapsodizes about Port-Royal's few decades of enchantment: "[I]t was a moment of unique perfection, which was necessarily transient. It was the coincident flowering of spirituality and genius which would wither when death removed the 'elite' souls whose conjunction formed its greatness."[19] Racine, the last "élite soul" of the Port-Royalists, died in 1699.[20]

The archenemies of the Port-Royalists were the Jesuits. Founded in 1534 as the Society of Jesus by the soldier-priest, Ignatius Loyola, this religious group was a recent addition to the Church's roster. One declaration of the order's charter singled them out from all other Catholic religious—a vow of absolute obedience to the Pope, and only the Pope. This stance immediately caused conflict when the Jesuits sought to establish themselves in France, due to the strong naive movement of Gallicanism. As a result, the Jesuits' first entrées into the country were not well received. One incident in particular derailed the early Jesuit cause. In 1594, a fanatical Catholic, educated by the Jesuits, attempted to kill King Henry IV of France.[21] By dint of association, the Jesuits were seen as condoning this act, leading to their eviction from French-controlled lands in 1595. The banishment only lasted a few years, and by 1603, they returned to France, regrouping and continuing their quest for authority.

The theological debate that raged between the Port-Royalists and the Jesuits revolved around the closely inter-woven and central issues of grace and predestination. While this disputation is too complex to address here in depth, it may be briefly summarized. In short, Augustine held that justification (defined as being freed or cleansed of sin) does not come by independent acts of the human will. Humans, by dint of original sin, are too degenerate to be capable of such faith. Justification, therefore, is the consequence of grace, and is a free gift from God.[22] Jansen, following in one strand of the Augustinian tradition, wrote that humankind is unable to influence to whom God dispenses grace and therefore salvation; this act is predestined and those who are not gifted with grace will be damned. Jansen strongly criticized the Jesuits for distorting the Church's true doctrine on this point, since the order preached, in his eyes, a partly Pelagian under-standing of grace.

Jansen and St. Cyran both advocated the Augustinian position that humanity is greatly depraved and their views on predestination are at times close to Calvin. Certain impulses connect Jansenism and Calvinism, including a common wish to return to what they saw as primitive Christianity, the weight they gave to human depravity and Augustinian theology, and the need for stringent moral behavior on the part of believers. While similarities exist between Calvinists and Jansenists, in the end the Jansenists remained committed to Roman Catholicism (although they advocated certain reforms) and held to the Church's sacramental theology as well as its other teachings.[23]

On the other hand, in opposition to the predestinarianism of the Jansenists, the Jesuits averred that grace and justification do not come about by faith alone—grace results from participation in the sacraments as well as good works. God offers these ways of attaining grace, and since humans possess free will, they may choose to engage in these actions. Although they could not disagree directly with Augustine, they redefined predestination to refer to God's foreknowledge of events, which still allowed for the agency of free will.[24]

Intent on gaining the upper hand in this argument, the Jesuits tried to block Jansen from publishing his book, *Augustinus*, which contained outright criticisms of their order. Although they cited legal and dogmatic reasons in their attempt to stay its publication, their efforts were unsuccessful. During this theological conflagration between Jansen and the Jesuits, St. Cyran, also an anti-Jesuit, rushed to his good friend's defense. In May 1638, the powerful French cardinal, Armand-Jean du Plessis, Duke de Richelieu (1585-1642), ordered the arrest of St. Cyran. In a further effort to undermine the Jansenists later that same year, Richelieu compelled the residents of Port-

Royal des Champs to vacate the compound, forcing them to relocate to Paris and elsewhere.

Over the objections of the Jesuits, *Augustinus* was published in 1640, two years after Jansen's death. St. Cyran languished in jail until the death of Richelieu in 1642. Although he obtained his release from captivity, the leader of the Port-Royalists died soon after, in 1643. Meanwhile, the Church and the crown continued and even stepped up the harassment of the recalcitrant Jansenists. By 1666, all the *petites écoles* were shuttered and a number of the convent's novices were forced to leave the abbey.[25]

In 1669, a compromise agreement called "The Peace of the Church" allowed a brief truce between the Church and the Jansenists. During the short lull in persecution, the Port-Royalists enjoyed a resurgence of popularity in religious and intellectual circles. The situation shifted dramatically with the death of the Duchess de Longueville[26] in 1679. Without the protection of their royal patron, the Jansenists became vulnerable targets once more, as the Church identified the Jansenists as subversives and Port-Royal as a nexus of rebellion. The Church ousted all the abbey's novices as well as any priests serving the community, and forbade Port-Royal to accept any new vocations.

How did the Catholic Church determine who was or was not a Jansenist? Often the Jesuits' accusations established who belonged to the enemy camp. Doyle wryly observes: "Jansenism was created by the Jesuits, in the sense that they used Jansen's name to stigmatize those who opposed them. A Jansenist, observed the Cistercian Cardinal Bona [1609-1674], was little more than a Catholic who disliked the Jesuits."[27]

Many of those indicted as Jansenists escaped from France during this time, often landing as refugees in the Netherlands. In 1679, immediately after the Duchess de Longueville's death, Antoine Arnauld sought refuge in the Netherlands, where he eventually died an exile. The Low Countries encouraged an attitude of religious toleration, unlike France, primarily because the Dutch considered such a stance to be a integral part of intelligent economics and political diplomacy.[28] Later, at the the height of Louis XIV's campaign against the Huguenots in 1685, the Dutch similarly offered a sanctuary to many persecuted French Protestants.

After the Jansenists fled to Holland, the Jesuits asked for the assistance of the Archbishop of Utrecht, Johannes van Neercassel (d. 1686), to round up the heretics and hand them over. He firmly rejected this proposition, and since the Netherlands was not a Catholic country, the Vatican had little effect in getting the Dutch government to assist them in arresting the Jansenists.[29] Seemingly frustrated by its inability to force the issue, Rome accused van Neercassel of being a heretic of the same color as the Jansenists he was protecting. In time, van Neercassel persuaded Rome he was not a Jansenist—he journeyed to the Vatican in 1670 to clear his name—and the accusations against him were dropped. Van Neercassel died in communion with Rome, the last archbishop of Utrecht to do so.[30]

Pieter Codde (1648-1710) succeeded van Neercassel as Archbishop of Utrecht. A native of Amsterdam, Codde received his education at the University of Louvain. In 1689, the Archbishop of Malines and the Bishops of Antwerp and Namur consecrated Codde as archbishop.

Unhappy with Codde's appointment and consecration, the Jesuits at Rome harassed him, charging that he was tainted with the heresies of Jansenism and Gallicanism. In reality, the main issue in the conflict between Utrecht and the Jesuits was not theological, but political and ecclesiological. Utrecht vehemently asserted its traditional rights of independence, and the Jesuits, as part of the Vatican's ongoing plan to centralize authority, tried to undermine the historic autonomy of the Dutch see. While Utrecht still claimed it had independence in certain local matters, based on the privileges bestowed on the diocese in the Middle Ages, the Jesuits argued that the ancient Chapter of Utrecht no longer existed as a result of the Reformation.

A papal commission set up by Innocent XII eventually cleared Codde of the charge of Jansenism. Nevertheless, due to a complex political situation, Rome suspended the archbishop in 1702, finally deposing him in 1704. The Vatican then appointed Theodore de Cock as the clergyman in charge of the administration of the Dutch dioceses. This action defied canon law, which states that bishops are entitled to a trial before they may be deposed. The Vatican gave Codde neither opportunity for due process nor any reason for his dismissal. After this controversial incident, Dutch Catholic community support was split between Codde and de Cock: the Chapters of Utrecht and Haarlem supported Codde.[31]

At the same time the rift was widening between Utrecht and Rome. France's King Louis XIV, realizing that the Jansenists were more powerful than he had realized, took measures to eradicate the group. Beginning in 1703, the king proceeded to systemically disband and destroy the abbey over the next few years, culminating in the razing of the buildings of Port-Royal and the demolition of the convent's cemetery in 1710. With the obliteration of the abbey complete, the government hoped to deter any pilgrims or physical monuments to the Jansenists, thereby blotting out the very memory of the Port-Royalists.[32]

To further suppress the Jansenists, Pope Clement XI, at the instigation of the Jesuits, condemned Jansen's *Augustinus* in the 1713 papal bull, *Unigenitus Dei Filius*. The bull contained 101 points of denunciation of Jansen and his theology, although most scholars agree that the bull largely misrepresented Jansen's conclusions. Thought to be one of the instigating factors in the French Revolution, this encyclical was so poorly composed that numerous groups in France protested against it, considering it a travesty. In the eyes of the Jansenists, the Enlightenment philosophes, and the members of the Paris *parlement* (local autonomous court), the document only confirmed the preposterousness of Rome. In this way, Jansenism became increasingly politicized, garnering broad support from a number of diverse contingencies.[33]

Part Three: European Mystical Currents Contemporaneous with Jansenism

In addition to Jansenism, two other European movements beleaguered Rome during the seventeenth century and early eighteenth centuries. Protestantism continued to be a great concern, and Pietism, the most significant movement in the history of Protestant spirituality, took root and flourished in northern and western Europe during this time. Furthermore, the Church was grappling with Quietism, a type of Catholic mysticism initially inspired by the writings of Spanish priest Miguel de

Molinos (1640-1696). At this point, a brief examination of these two spiritual currents and their relationship to Jansenism would be helpful in understanding the milieu in which St. Cyran preached.

Beginning with Pietism, we see that although a homogenous movement never existed, its adherents generally held certain essential ideas in common: a judgmental view of Church dogma, polity, and services; members highly dedicated to self reflection and close study of the Bible; and a detachment from worldly affairs.[34] Pietists undercut Church authority by declaring that all true Christians are called to mystic union, while "false" Christians were embroiled in the institutional hidebound, and legalistic Church.[35] This stream of interiority crossed ecclesial boundaries and influenced Catholic spirituality as well, including, to an extent, Jansenism.[36] While differing on sacramental theology, both Pietists and Jansenists stressed the necessity of repentance and being reborn in Christ as well as great personal sanctity, and complete abandonment to God's will. Church reform and Bible study in the vernacular were important facets of both movements.

Quietist spirituality and its modified form, Semi-Quietism, thrived in Europe, especially France and Italy, between the late seventeenth and early eighteenth centuries. First clearly limned out by de Molinos, Quietest theology minimized the import of redemption and the salvific role of Jesus.[37] Its adherents placed high worth on individual contemplation and the soul's utter surrender to God. In doing so, its enthusiasts devalued of corporate and outward spiritual activities, including participation in the sacraments and good works. In the view of the Quietists, moreover, such doings might be harmful in that the soul might be distracted from its merging with God. The Semi-Quietist teachings of Madame Jeanne de la Mothe Guyon (1648-1717) articulate a monism in which the soul "disappears" into God through passive contemplation, no longer existing as a separate entity in relation to the Divine.[38]

All three of the above groups lessened the importance of priestly mediation, believing that the worshipper may relate to God directly. One outcome of this belief was a high ratio of women participants in these forms of spirituality, buoyed by the contention that prayer and the sanctification of daily life could be pursued equally by both sexes. Female founders and leaders of these movements existed in significant numbers, including Mère Angélique Arnauld of the Port-Royalists and Madame Guyon.[39]

While Quietists and Jansenists differed theologically in certain ways, they both saw a need for reform within the Catholic Church and shared a common enemy in the Jesuits. In the case of Quietism, the Jesuit and Dominican orders joined forces to persecute its advocates, specifically de Molinos and Guyon; Rome eventually condemned their teachings. In quashing Quietism (and one might add, Jansenism), Kolakowski avers that the Roman Catholic Church adversely affected Catholic mysticism for many years into the future.[40]

Part Four: The Schism between the Dutch Catholics and Rome

It was not until after Codde's death in December 1710 that Rome took its retribution on the Dutch Catholics for refusing to hand over the Jansenists. When the See of

Utrecht requested permission to elect a new archbishop, Rome refused to consent. Moreover, Rome argued that it had the right to dissolve the Utrecht diocese and declare it a mission. As a consequence of the Vatican's position and the stalemate between Rome and the Dutch Catholics, Holland had no bishop for a number of years. During those years, Dutch candidates to the priesthood traveled to Ireland, where the Bishop of Meath ordained them.[41]

Enter Dominique-Marie Varlet, the Catholic prelate and devoted missionary who had been in charge of the French missionary effort in the region called "Louisiana" since 1712. At the time, Louisiana was a huge geographical area of the North American colonies analogous to the present-day midwestern region of the United States. Moss reports that it consisted of "the vast region beyond the Alleghany Mountains, from Lake Superior to the Gulf of Mexico."[42]

In 1718 or 1719, Varlet journeyed to Québec in order to report to his bishop, after which he planned to return to his missionary work in Louisiana. Before leaving Québec, however, he received a letter from Rome instructing him to go to Paris and become consecrated, then continue on to Persia, where he would take up the office of the coadjucator bishop of Babylon. On 19 February 1719 in Paris, three Roman Catholic bishops privately consecrated Varlet as the Bishop of Ascalon. On the very day of his consecration, Varlet took delivery of another missive from Rome, informing him that he was now the bishop of Babylon, due to the fact that the former bishop had died on November 20, 1718.[43]

Varlet left Paris for Babylon in March 1719, following the Vatican's order to travel incognito. As he made his way through Holland, church officials in the diocese of Utrecht asked him to confirm 604 children during Easter week. There had been no bishop in the Low Countries since Archbishop Codde was suspended in 1702. While some Dutch children were sent abroad during this period to receive the sacrament, these particular children in question were either orphans or those whose parents were too impoverished to send them travelling for confirmation. Varlet agreed to confirm the Dutch children and afterwards continued his trek through Europe and Russia, arriving in Persia in October 1719.[44]

His tenure as bishop of Babylon was short-lived. In March 1720, Rome informed him that he was being suspended from the episcopate. The Vatican charged, among other infractions, that Varlet was not authorized to perform episcopal roles such as confirmation in the Netherlands. Although Varlet tried to have his suspension revoked, he did not help his cause by refusing to: 1) agree to the principles outlined in the bull *Unigenitus Dei Filius*; 2) give up his diocese of Babylon; or 3) apologize for confirming the children of Utrecht. Varlet relocated to Amsterdam and continued to campaign to have his suspension rescinded, even though a canon lawyer whose advice he sought out warned that the case was hopeless.[45]

In April 1723, realizing that Rome was not going to approve another bishop for Utrecht, the cathedral chapter of the diocese elected Cornelius Steenoven (d. 1725) as archbishop. Although the chapter implored Rome to sanction this action, no answer came from the Holy See. Rome did react after Varlet consecrated Steenoven as archbishop in October 1724 by excommunicating the newly elevated prelate in 1725.[46]

The election and consecration of Steenoven marked the beginning of the independent Dutch Catholic Church. Steenoven died two months after Benedict's excommunication and Varlet consecrated Cornelius John Barchman Wuytiers (d. 1733) as Archbishop of Utrecht in September 1725.[47] In line with its treatment of Steenoven, Rome routinely excommunicated each new archbishop of Utrecht.[48] Although Rome did away with its censure of the See of Utrecht after Vatican II, no reconciliation has taken place between the two churches. Pius IX reinstituted a Roman Catholic presence in Holland in March 1853 and today the Old Catholic Church of the Netherlands still exists side-by-side with the Roman Catholic Church in the Dutch republic (now a monarchy).[49]

Part Five: Vatican I and the Origins of the Old Catholic Church

One hundred and sixty-five years later, the Dutch Catholic Church joined with the Old Catholic movement, a reform group of Roman Catholics that developed in the German-speaking countries of Western Europe during the First Vatican Council. In 1869, the Roman Catholic Church held a church-wide council, Vatican I. One of the decisions made by the council was to approve the doctrine of papal infallibility. A group of Roman Catholic dissenters, many of them professors and theologians, strongly objected to this new doctrine. The protestors, who primarily hailed from Germany, Switzerland, and Austria, contended that papal infallibility was a theological and historical deviation from Church teachings and tradition. The principal instigator of this revolt against Rome was

Johann Friedrich von Shulte (1827-1914), a professor of canon law at the University of Prague. Von Shulte protested vociferously against the new dogma handed down by Vatican I and even questioned its validity as an ecumenical council.[50] Johann Joseph Ignaz von Döllinger (1799-1890), a highly respected priest and professor of canon law and church history, was another leader in the dispute. This opposition movement coined the term "Old Catholic" to differentiate them from what they saw as the new and heterodox Roman Catholicism promulgated by Vatican I. In the end, the Vatican Council overruled the activists' objections and the newly defined doctrines became Church dogma. Although the protestors did not wish to form a separate religious body, their consciences did not allow them to acquiesce to Rome. Beginning in 1873, a number of these dissenting Roman Catholics formed separate Old Catholic churches in their respective countries.[51] Von Döllinger, although a leader in the revolt, did not officially join the Old Catholic movement. He was, however, publicly sympathetic with its establishment. He steadfastly refused to submit to Rome on the matters of papal infallibility and the Immaculate Conception of Mary, and Rome responded by defrocking and excommunicating him in 1871. Von Döllinger died in 1890 and his funeral was held in an Old Catholic Church; he never reconciled with the Vatican, despite many entreaties from the Roman Catholic Church.[52]

The Dutch Catholic Church of Utrecht consecrated bishops for the newly constituted Old Catholics in order that they might have the properly ordained clergy with which to form an autocephalous church body. By 1889, the Old Catholic churches and the Dutch Catholic

Church came to be known collectively as "Old Catholics" as they united behind the Declaration of Utrecht, which defined their unified doctrinal foundation. The Declaration "accepts the teachings of the primitive church as the ecumenical councils down to A.D. 1000 define them, and affirms the sacrifice of the Mass and the real presence of Christ in the sacrament of the altar.... It rejects the dogmas of the immaculate conception of the Blessed Virgin Mary and papal infallibility...."[53]

Old Catholicism was solely a European phenomenon until the French priest, Joseph René Vilatte, brought this tradition to the United States. The next chapter will limn out Vilatte's singular ecclesial history.

Chapter Two
Joseph René Vilatte and the French Independent Esoteric Catholic Churches of the Nineteenth and Early Twentieth Centuries

Part One: *La Petite Église* and Joseph Henry Vilatte

During the nineteenth century, religious controversy once again agitated the country of France, as had been true for much of its history. Before the Revolution of 1789, French society had been stratified for centuries in three orders or estates. Roman Catholic clergy comprised the *premier état* (first estate) and the Church owned 10% of the land. Duties of the first estate included registering births, marriages, and deaths, administering hospitals and schools, and collecting the *dîme*, a tithe of usually 10%. Jews and Protestants were not allowed to worship publicly or hold public office. The nobility formed the second estate, while the vast majority of the French fell into the third estate, including merchants and peasants.

In 1790, the French National Assembly took steps to deracinate the Church's hegemony by reducing the number of dioceses by almost half (from 137 to 80) and auctioning off most of Church-owned land to the highest bidder. Under this new plan, the government also abolished the collection of Church tithes. Instead, the state took charge of paying clergy salaries (who were now to be elected to their posts) and maintaining church buildings. Most distressingly to the Church, the revolutionary government declared that all Roman Catholic clergy take vows of allegiance to the state. In Rome, Pope Pius VI fulminated against this legislation and the gutting of papal authority over the French church.[1] Reprisal from the Vatican came in the form of three briefs, the last in 1792: "After appealing to the clergy and people of France not to cooperate with *les intrus*...[i]n March 1792 Pius excommunicated all ecclesiastics who accepted the provisions of the C.C.C. [Civil Constitution of the Clergy] and all Catholics who cooperated with the constitutional clergy."[2]

Only four of 131 bishops disregarded the Pope's proclamation and rose to support the government in its aim to organize a French church independent of Rome. This quartet formed the backbone of the governmentally sanctioned Constitutional Church. As the Constitutional Church gained congregants, several more priests were raised to the episcopate by the schismatic bishops. Over 1,600 priests fled into exile rather than capitulate to the National Assembly's demands, but many others stayed; those acquiescing clergy, comprising about 50% of French priests, became known as "jurors." After a tumultuous decade in which even the Constitutional clergy often squared off against the government, Napoleon and Pope Pius VII agreed on a treaty known as the 1801 Concordat, officially signed in 1802. This pact ameliorated some of the earlier anti-cleric tension of the revolutionary era, but

Bonaparte's government maintained the status quo in regard to the land distribution legislated by the National Assembly—lands seized during the Revolution would not be returned to the French church. It also upheld civil rights and religious toleration for Protestants and Jews; heresy and blasphemy were no longer considered civil crimes. Not only Catholic clergy but Jews and Protestant clergy also received state support, even though the Concordat formally acknowledged Catholicism as the majority faith. At this time, most of the Constitutional Church bishops, previously excommunicated, submitted to Pius VII, and were allowed to retain their posts.[3] Realistically, although anti-cleric parties and some Catholics opposed it, the Concordat brought a measure of peace to the nation.

The Concordat rankled a few thousand Constitutional Church congregants, including a handful of bishops, who refused to accept the Concordat and submit to Rome. Some of this dissatisfaction may have been due to the deathblow dealt to Gallicanism by the Concordat.[4] Eventually this dissident group evolved into a discrete sect called the *Petite Église*. Although the church's last archbishop died in 1829 without appointing a successor and its last priest died in 1847, it continued with baptisms carried out by laymen and its members became known as "the Incommunicants,"[5] due to their lack of clergy. Anson reports that in 1903 the *Petite Église* tried to unite with the Old Catholic Church of Utrecht, although nothing came of it.[6]

Fittingly, one of the singular figures of modern independent Catholicism, Joseph René Vilatte, was raised within the *Petite Église* community. Vilatte was born in

Paris in 1854. Ansor states that his parents had him baptized in the *Petite Église*; Thériault writes that it was Vilatte's paternal grandparents who were active in the independent Catholic sect.[7] His mother died when he was three years old and eventually Vilatte's father sent him to live in the Parisian orphanage run by the Roman Catholic order, *Frères des Écoles Chrétiennes* (F.É.C., Brothers of the Christian Schools). The brothers had him confirmed in 1867 in the Notre Dame Cathedral in Paris and subsequently trained him as a teacher.[8]

At the young age of 16, Vilatte joined up with the Garde National to fight in the Franco-Prussian War. Soon after his discharge in 1871, he journeyed to Canada and obtained a position as a teacher at the St. Anthony School in Ottawa. Eventually Vilatte joined the F.É.C and traveled to Belgium in 1877 to begin his novitiate. A few months later, he returned to Canada and enrolled in a Catholic college in Montreal to study philosophy. In 1880, while a student in Montreal he met Father Charles Chiniquy, who became his most important mentor.[9]

Father Charles Chiniquy (1809-1899) established the French-Canadian Community Movement in the mid-nineteenth century (incorporated in the United States as the Christian Catholic Church) and ministered to French Canadians living in Canada and the United States. A native Canadian, he began his lifelong clerical career in 1833 at the age of 24, when he was ordained as a Roman Catholic priest. In 1852 he was transferred to the Diocese of Chicago, where he established St. Anne's French-Canadian Roman Catholic Church. Because he insisted on saying Mass in French as well as focusing on the Bible more than on the Church's magisterium, he ran afoul of the diocesan leadership. The Roman Catholic leadership insisted that parishioners use English in church services as well as in religious schools and demanded that Chiniquy comply with their policy. To Chiniquy and his parishioners at St. Anne's parish, self-determination and preservation of French language and culture were paramount concerns. When Chiniquy and the parish refused to obey the diocese's demand, the bishop of Chicago excommunicated him, ostensibly for doctrinal errors. In 1858 his parish followed him out of the church of Rome and "proclaimed themselves Catholics of Christ," which gave rise to the moniker, "Christian Catholics."[10]

A strong advocate of ecumenism, Chiniquy joined the interdenominational Protestant *Société missionnaire canadienne-française* (SMCF) in 1875. Chiniquy and his followers then affiliated with the Presbyterian Church, although they were allowed to maintain their autonomy as a church and were not forced to accept the Presbyterian Westminster Confession of Faith. In 1880, Chiniquy happened to be lecturing in Montreal, when Vilatte, at the time a student at College de Saint Laurent, attended a number of his talks on "Roman errors." Convinced to leave the Roman Catholic Church by Chiniquy's arguments, Vilatte then took up theological studies at the French Theology department of the Presbyterian College of McGill University in 1881 for two years to prepare for the ministry, with the encouragement of Chiniquy.[11]

In 1883, Vilatte traveled to Chicago to study with Chiniquy and joined the Church of St. Anne. By 1884, Vilatte was toiling diligently as a Presbyterian missionary in Wisconsin among French-speaking immigrants, a task that was sometimes accompanied by physical hardships as well as social ostracism, the latter due to the lack of interest in Protestantism demonstrated by most of the area's Belgians and French immigrants in the area.[12] In 1884, Vilatte was able to establish a "Christian Catholic" church for the Francophones in Green Bay, Wisconsin. In Vilatte's eyes, this church was a community house of worship that accepted all Christians without qualification. Most of the parishioners of this new church were Roman Catholic but were without pastoral guidance since the Roman Catholic diocese of Green Bay rarely sent clergy to minister to these French-speaking parishioners. Eventually Vilatte gained an enthusiastic following and a reputation as a talented and charismatic preacher.

In order to deal with this complicated pastoral situation in which a Protestant missionary guided a Roman Catholic flock, Chiniquy suggested that Vilatte write to Charles (Père Hyacinthe) Loyson (1827-1912), a former Roman Catholic priest who headed the independent Gallican church in France. Through a series of intercontinental communiqués, Loyson recommended to Edward Herzog, the Old Catholic Bishop of Switzerland, that Vilatte be ordained to the Old Catholic priesthood. The young priest's status in the community impressed John Henry Hobert Brown, the Anglican bishop of Fond du Lac, Wisconsin, who agreed to oversee and assist Vilatte's missionary work within his diocese. In fact, Bishop Brown wrote a letter to Bishop Herzog, recommending Vilatte for ordination. In order to prepare for his ordination, Vilatte underwent "theological retraining" at the Episcopalian Nashotah House Seminary in Wisconsin. He then traveled to Switzerland and was tutored by Professor Eugene Michaud of the University of Berne in order that he might pass the qualifying exams given by the Christian (Old) Catholic Faculty of Theology at that university. Satisfied with Vilatte's preparation, Herzog ordained Vilatte as an Old Catholic deacon and priest in June 1885 in Berne.[13]

Returning to the States, Vilatte founded a mission called *Bon Pasteur* (Good Shepherd) in Little Sturgeon, Wisconsin, in 1885, under the protection of Brown. By 1886, the mission evolved into a permanent church, which was dedicated by Brown on 20 September 1887. During these years, Vilatte expanded his mission to other areas of Wisconsin, as well as Ontario and Québec.[14]

During this time, certain leaders in the Episcopal Church were attempting to position their denomination as "The American Catholic Church."[15] Bishop Brown thought that this collaboration with Vilatte would encourage a positive relationship between the Old Catholics and the Episcopal Church, who were both at odds with the Vatican.[16] The Episcopalians may have seen Vilatte's ordination to the Old Catholic priesthood as way of both attracting Francophones to their denomination as well as introducing valid (from a Roman Catholic perspective) orders into their denomination, in the event that any potential converts (or even current Episcopalians) had doubts about the validity of the Anglican connection to the apostolic succession.[17]

Vilatte's mission in Wisconsin and Canada flourished under Brown; it is unclear however if he took formal vows of obedience to Brown at his ordination to the priesthood.[18] Between 1886 and 1889, Vilatte worked industriously, gathering supporters and successfully touring the East Coast to raise money for his mission.[19] By 1889, he felt that he was ready to assume the Old Catholic episcopate. He had the support of his parishioners and may have been well qualified for the position; nonetheless, this proposed consecration threatened to set off financial and political problems between the diocese of Fond du Lac and the Old Catholic Church in Europe.

Bishop Brown died on 2 May 1888 and was succeeded by Bishop Charles Grafton, whose authoritarian style of management differed greatly from his predecessor's more laissez faire attitude. Grafton wanted to centralize authority and have the Francophone churches under Vilatte to reassign their property titles to the Episcopal diocese. In reaction to Grafton's demands, Vilatte's parishioners convened a synod in Wisconsin. This synod elected Vilatte the first bishop of the Christian Catholic Rite of Community Churches (CCRCC) on 16 November 1889.[20]

Following his election, Vilatte approached the Old Catholic Church for consecration as a bishop. His request was refused, very possibly as a result of Grafton's campaign to discredit Vilatte with the Old Catholic Church. Thériault posits that by damaging Vilatte's reputation, Grafton hoped that the French priest's followers would desert him and come under Grafton's administrative control, along with the buildings and land of the Christian Catholic Church.[21] For Grafton's part, his autobiography records that he did not believe that Vilatte was "either morally or intellectually fitted for the office [of bishop]." Historian William Hogue is of the opinion that, "[w]hat really drove Grafton to his relentless harassment of Vilatte can only be guessed at, but there is little doubt that he did contribute mightily to the refusal of recognition, not only by the Anglican churches, but by the European Old

Catholics and by the Roman Church as well. The Vilatte "Old Catholics" consequently remained a small sect, constantly splintering into rival factions...under a cloud of suspected fraud as well as ecclesiastical illegitimacy."[22]

Vilatte then approached a Russian Orthodox bishop for consecration, without success. Finally in July 1891, Vilatte traveled by steamer to Southeast Asia, using $225.00 that his supporters raised to provide him with a ticket and food.[23] On 29 May 1892, at the Church of Our Lady of Good Death in Colombo, Ceylon, he received consecration at the hands of three bishops in the Syrian-Jacobite apostolic succession who were prelates in the Independent Catholic Church of Ceylon, India, and Goa: Mar Julius (Colombo, Ceylon), Mar Athanasius (Kottayam, India) and Mar Gregorius (Niranan, India).

Upon his return to the United States, the new bishop vigorously exercised his episcopal office, ordaining priests and consecrating bishops in large numbers to minister in various states, including Massachusetts, Illinois, Minnesota, Wisconsin, New York, and also abroad in Canada and Haiti. In 1893, Vilatte accepted the position of Grand Master in the Order of the Crown of Thorns (OCT), a fraternal and chivalrous society of men and women founded in 1891 by Episcopal priest, Gaston Fercken (1855-1930). The goals of the OCT are "to reward those who believe in the God Man, Jesus Christ, and appreciating the grand priviledge [sic] of the Christian Faith, heroically propagate its doctrines and combat error under whatever form it may present itself. The Order also has in view to recompense piety, humility and philanthropy wheresoever they may be found."[24] Order members initiated by Vilatte included Paolo

Miraglia-Guilotti (1357-1918), Julien-Ernest Houssaye (1844-1912), and Jean Bricaud (1881-1934), all of whom Vilatte also ordained or consecrated as independent Catholic prelates.[25]

In the summer of 1898, Vilatte began a European sabbatical, which included a meeting in London with Dr. Frederick G. Lee, the head of the Order of Corporate Reunion. Vilatte resided in Paris in 1900 and his home included a chapel in which he performed priestly ordinations.[26] In May 1900, he consecrated the Italian Paolo Miraglia-Gulotti, a former Roman Catholic priest; on 13 June 1900, the Roman Catholic Church excommunicated both Vilatte and Miraglia-Gulotti. Later that year, Vilatte returned to the United States. By 1904, he returned to France, having been asked to help restore the Gallican church.[27] For several years, off and on, Vilatte ministered in France, a period that will be examined more closely in Part Five of this chapter.

Vilatte returned to the States in 1908 and ministered actively until 1923, when he decided to retire to France. He spent the remainder of his years as an ascetic, moving to a cottage on the grounds of a Roman Catholic monastery in Versailles in 1925. Joseph René Vilatte died on 1 July 1929 and conflicting reports of his last days abound.[28] His sympathetic biographer Serge Thériault (currently presiding bishop of Vilatte's Christian Catholic Church) records that the monastery authorities allowed Vilatte to wear episcopal vestments and that he was respectfully addressed as *monseigneur*. Thériault makes no mention of Vilatte's alleged formal acquiescence to the Roman faith and includes a photograph of Vilatte's memorial stone in a Versailles graveyard, which reads, "In

Memoriam, Msgr. J. Rene Vilatte, 1854-1929, 1st bishop,
Christian Catholic Church, Canada and USA."[29] Another
biography of Vilatte categorically states that, "Contrary to
what most Independent Catholic writers say, he was not
buried a layperson but with full honour and dignity of a
Church Bishop. Abbot Janssens of the Cistercian
monastery ordered that he lie in state in his episcopal
vestments and mitred."[30]

Anson disputes the fact that Vilatte was allowed to wear
episcopal dress and furthermore states that Vilatte did
reenter the Roman Catholic Church, although questions
the sincerity of that reconciliation. While Anson charac-
terizes Vilatte as a "buccaneer ecclesiastical adventurer"
and "an utterly unstable Frenchman," the bishop's supporters envision him as a saintly and valiant defender of
the people in the struggle against church authoritarian-
ism. Without a doubt, Joseph Rene Vilatte remains an
enigmatic and remarkable figure in the history of
Independent Catholicism and one who is able to conjure
up strong emotions even to this day.[31]

Vilatte's consecrators in Ceylon belonged to an independent Catholic lineage that split from the Roman
Catholic Church in 1887-1888. The new independent
church then successfully petitioned Mar Ignatius Peter III,
Jacobite Patriarch of Antioch, to be accepted into the
Syrian Orthodox Church. Thus, those bishops and priests
ordained and consecrated *only* in the Vilatte lineage are
not strictly speaking Old Catholics in terms of historical
lineage but rather are in the Syrian-Jacobite succession.[32]
However, contemporary independent sacramental priests
and bishops in the United States almost universally hold
the lineages of *both* Vilatte and of Arnold Harris Mathew

(1852-1919), an English Old Catholic bishop (whose story is limned out in Chapter Three); therefore, those priests *are* directly connected to the Old Catholic succession. Another lineage that eventually joined forces with that of Vilatte's is the nineteenth-century French Gnostics, whose fascinating tale is told in Part Two.

Part Two: *L'Église Johannites des Chrétiens Primitifs* and *Œuvre de la Misericorde*

Before this study maps out the history of the French Gnostic churches of the late nineteenth and early twentieth centuries, it will be helpful to examine two early nineteenth-century esoteric independent French Catholic movements, both of whose lineages eventually joined up with the Gnostic lineage inaugurated by Jules Doinel (1842-1902) in 1890.

The first is *l'Église Johannites des Chrétiens Primitifs*, a church that traces its origins back to the reviving of the Knights Templar in 1804 by several Frenchmen, including former Roman Catholic priest Bernard Fabré-Palaprat (1777-1838).[33] The *Ordre du Temple* (Order of the Templars) declared that it was an extension of the medieval Catholic religious order dissolved by Pope Clement V in 1312. The nineteenth-century revitalized order developed into a quasi-Catholic group with Masonic membership as a prerequisite to church membership. Eventually church polity developed to include a primate and a patriarch, as well as ordained priests, known as "Doctors of the Law," who facilitated the church's private ceremonies. Numerous lapsed Roman Catholic clergy were members, including Msg. Mauviel (1757-1814) and Fabré-Palaprat, who co-founded *l'Église*

Johannites des Chrétiens Primitifs in 1828. Both men were also prominent Masons.[34]

According to "oral tradition," Fabré-Palaprat came upon a two-part manuscript purporting to be a version of the Gospel of John, which he purchased second-hand in a Parisian bookstore in 1814. He eventually based the philosophy of the revived Order of the Templars on this manuscript. Envisioning himself as an inheritor of an apostolic lineage originating with St. John, he disseminated the idea common among esoteric Christians: that of two branches of the Church, one inner—the Church of St. John—and the outer Church of St. Peter. In Fabré-Palaprat's conception, the esoteric church of St. John catered to those spiritually advanced souls who might comprehend Jesus' secret teachings, while the exoteric Church of St. Peter accommodated the masses. After Fabré-Palaprat's death, the Order of the Templars was divided between those who championed *l'Église Johannites des Chrétiens Primitifs* (also referred to as the Johannine Church) and those who resisted its continuation.[35]

Msg. Ferdinand Chatel (1795-1857) carried on the Fabré-Palaprat line while deemphasizing the Masonic and occult nature of the mother church. A Roman Catholic priest and fervent Gallican, he established a schismatic chapel in Paris in 1831 and received ordination in the *l'Église Johannites des Chrétiens Primitifs* a few months later. In due course Mgr. Machault, the primate of the *l'Église Johannites des Chrétiens Primitifs*, raised Chatel to bishop. Chatel officially established his Gallican church, *l'Église Catholique Française*, in 1833, which in time launched small communities in both France and Belgium. In the early 1840s both civil and church authorities worked to suppress Chatel's sect and King Louis-Philippe, who reigned from 1830 to 1848, succeeded in this undertaking. After 1860, the church is rarely heard of.[36]

Pierre-Eugène-Michel Vintras (1807-1875), a French layman from the town of Bayeaux, founded another esoterically oriented church in 1839. That year, Vintras, the manager of a cardboard factory, had a prophetic vision: the Holy Mother, St. Joseph, and the angels told him to begin a movement under the name *Œuvre de la Misericorde* (Work of Mercy) "to herald the coming of the Paraclete."[37] Similar to the medieval mystic Joachim de Fiore, Vintras sermonized that the "Reign of the Suffering Christ" was at its end and the advent of the "Reign of the Holy Spirit of Love" was on the horizon. The movement quickly expanded due to Vintras' vigorous traveling and preaching, with a number of Roman Catholic priests joining him. The prophet's charisma and the miracles attributed to him drew many congregants in a brief time. According to some accounts, supernatural events followed in Vintras' wake: "Stigmata, bleeding hosts, glossolalia, visions: no spiritual experience, however extreme or unusual, seems to have been foreign to the Œuvre de la Miséricorde."[38]

Vintras' popularity drew the ire of Church and governmental authorities, and he was arrested around 1843 and thrown in jail for several years on a charge of theft. Fueling the authorities' displeasure was the fact that a number of Vintras's devotees were extreme royalists who supported the controversial and ultimately unsuccessful campaign of Karl Wilhelm Nauncorff (d. 1845) who claimed to be Louis VXII, heir to the French throne.[39] By 1844 Pope Gregory XVI had condemned the *Œuvre de la Miséricorde*.[40]

After his release from jail in 1848, Vintras had another vision in which Christ consecrated him and instructed him in a new vernacular liturgy. As bishop, he raised seven Roman Catholic priests to the Œuvre de la Misericorde episcopate and they in turn consecrated him. By 1852, the fact that Vintras' church congregation continued to swell alarmed both civil and Church authorities. That year the French monarch Louis-Napoleon (1808-1873) gave the order that the church be disbanded.[41]

Hounded in France, Vintras immigrated to Belgium while a number of his followers fled France and established Œuvre de la Misericorde groups in England, Italy, and Spain. In 1863 Vintras returned to France and two years later established a sanctuary at Lyons, called le santuaire intériuer du Carmel d' Elie—therefore the later incarnation of Vintras' church, which expanded to other parts of western Europe including Florence, is often known as the Church of Carmel.[42]

The renowned occultist Eliphas Levi (Alphonse Louis Constant, 1810-1875) called on Vintras several times during Vintras' exile in England. Levi reflected that, "Vintras is an illiterate labourer, but gifted with a singular fluidic power. He reflects immediately the spirit of any person who comes to him and reproduces on the spot the thought of people he is seeing for the first time."[43] Levi also recounted his interactions with the abbé La Charvoz,[44] a leader in the Œuvre de la Misericorde who related to Levi some amazing miracles that occurred in the Vintrasian Church. Indeed, Levi was astonished when Abbé La Charvoz, upon Levi's insistence, showed him Eucharistic wafers that had become miraculously soaked with blood during a Mass.[45]

After Vintras died in 1875, former Roman Catholic priest Joseph-Antoine Boullan (1824-1893), known as the Abbé de Boullan, took over the stewardship of the church. La Charvoz and Abbé Héry assisted Boullan, who was infamous for his religio-sexual practices. Under the new bishop's guidance, the church evolved into an increasingly occult and spiritualistic movement.[46]

Part Three: Jules Doinel
and *l'Église Gnostique de France*

In the 1890s, the city of Paris offered a vital and liberated environment for artists, writers, poets, playwrights, and the politically defiant. Although *fin de siècle* Paris had its dilemmas and dangers, including frequent bombings by anarchist groups, the capital presented its denizens and visitors a freedom of expression and creation that could hardly be rivaled in Europe. Not surprisingly, therefore, Paris became the hub of a major occult resurgence, one that attracted a wide swathe of the French population: "The renewed interest in the occult was by no means confined to a few eccentrics and scholars and it was inevitable that artists and poets who had turned from naturalism to the world of dreams and the mysteries of the spirit should include magic in their sphere of interests. A wider public which avidly read accounts of new scienic [sic] marvels was also becoming fascinated again by supernatural subjects."[47] Pope Leo XIII, possibly alarmed by the upsurge of interest in occultism, promulgated the 20 April 1884 encyclical, *Humanum Genum*, which censured Freemasons as perverse and evil miscreants who wielded a pernicious influence within society. After publication of this bull, Roman Catholics became subject to excommunication for joining Masonic lodges.[48]

The occult craze manifested in the formation of esoteric sects as well as an explosion of books on magic, sorcery, mysticism, Kabbalah, alchemy, and Satanism. The leading occult writer of the time, Eliphas Lévi, had great success with his renowned tomes, *Dogma et ritual de la haute magie* (*Dogma and Ritual of High Magic*, 1856) and *Histoire de la magie* (*History of Magic*, 1860). Formerly a deacon in the Roman Catholic Church, he came in contact with Martinism and became an avid supporter of Louis-Claude Saint-Martin's philosophy, though Lévi remained a devoted Catholic throughout his life. (Saint-Martin's work and influence will be explored in Part Seven of this chapter.)[49]

Jules Doinel (Jules-Benoît Stanislaus Doinel de Val-Michel, 1842–1902), a frequent denizen of spiritualistic and occult organizations including the Masons and the Swedenborgian Church, launched the modern Gnostic movement in France. In 1888, while immersed in studies of the Cathars and the Bogomils, Doinel had a vision of the "Eon Jesus," who consecrated him as "Bishop of Montségur and Primate of the Albigenses." In this revelation, Eon Jesus commanded the newly ordained bishop to found a Gnostic church.[50]

While most of the churches examined in this book are bound together by their claim to apostolic succession through the laying on of hands by a bishop, Doinel was consecrated through an inner contact with Jesus, just as Vintras claimed to be. Such a phenomenon is not as strange as it may initially appear when considering the context of esotericism. Plummer explains that, "As esotericism has an explicit openness to interchange with beings on other levels of reality, the idea of a new priesthood coming from such inner contact is not as much of a stretch as it might otherwise be."[51] Léonce-Eugène Fabre des Essarts, later ordained to the episcopate by Doinel, discussed this controversial beginning of Doinel's church in his book, *L'Arbre Gnostique* (1899). He notes that when Tau[52] Valentinus II (Doinel's religious name, which honored the early Gnostic Christian teacher Valentinus) appeared to preach to the new era of Gnosis to people of goodwill, skeptics asked who was his consecrator. "Valentinus II might have followed the example of Fabré-Palaprat, the founder of an alleged Templar religion, and claim a sacerdotal filiation to Simon [Magus] or Cerinthus.[53] But he preferred to state the truth, that 'It was the Eon Jesus himself who imposed his hands upon me and consecrated me bishop of Montségur.'"[54]

In a series of later séances, held at the palatial home of Lady Marie Caithness (1830-1895)[55] in Paris, Doinel was contacted by a synod of thirteenth-century Cathar bishops headed by Guihabert de Castres, who was martyred at Montségur in 1244. During one séance, Doinel received this message from a spirit claiming to be "Sophia-Achamôth:"

> I address myself to you because you are
> my friend, my servant and the prelate of my
> Albigensian Church. I am exiled from the
> Pleroma, and it is I whom Valentinus named
> Sophia-Achamôth. It is I whom Simon
> Magus called Helene-Ennoia; for I am the
> Eternal Androgyne. Jesus is the Word of
> God; I am the Thought of God. One day I
> shall return to my Father above, but I
> require assistance in this; to intercede for
> me, the supplications of my Brother Jesus

are required. Only the Infinite is able to redeem the Infinite, and only God is able to redeem God. Listen well: The One has brought forth One, then One. And the Three are but One: the Father, the Word and the Thought. Establish my Gnostic Church. The Demiurge will be powerless against it. Receive the Paraclete."[56]

The two medieval groups that Doinel had been researching, the Bogomils and the Cathars, have a controversial and fascinating history. The Bogomils, a dualistic Christian church that flourished between the tenth and fifteenth centuries in the Balkans, drew their teachings from Gnostic, Manichean, and Paulician traditions.[57] The Cathars were a dissident Gnostic Christian sect active in southern and western Europe between the mid-twelfth and early fourteenth centuries. Bogomil and Cathar rites and doctrine are comparable in numerous ways, although scholars have not been able to clearly establish the relationship between the two groups.

Only a few primary Cathar documents survive—most of what is known about the sect derives from the writings of medieval heresiologists and inquisitors. Edina Bozoky identifies two main ideological Cathar streams: the first is the "absolute dualism" advocated by the Cathars of the Languedoc (southern France), in which the spiritual, pure, and invisible realm of God is juxtaposed from the beginning of time to the Satanic material world of darkness and evil. The more moderate Cathars (primarily in Italy) believed that the One God created both worlds and that the prideful angel Satan, was cast out of heaven and received dominion over the nascent material world. All

Cathars, though, held that humans are fallen angels trapped in human bodies. In order to escape this material realm and return to God, they sought to avoid worldly contamination as much as possible.[58]

Lambert notes that the Cathar faithful, like those in many dualistic sects, were divided into two distinct groups: the Perfects (*Parfait*), the monastic elite, and the Believers, the laity. The Parfait consisted of a select group of both men and women who had submitted to the *consolamentum*, the sacrament in which they embraced strict ascetic vows and became fully initiated members of the Cathar Church. Lambert avers, "The Cathar ritual of the *consolamentum* derives from the Bogomil form of the initiation of adepts."[59]

The Believers, on the other hand, were allowed to consume meat as well as marry and procreate (although the Cathar Church opposed procreation as a general principle, repulsed by the idea of imprisoning more fallen angels in human bodies). The Perfects traveled the countryside, usually in pairs, preaching the faith and administering the *consolamentum* to those laity deemed ready for the rigors of the fully committed Cathar life.[60]

Cathar beliefs, transmitted for the most part orally and therefore subject to a fair amount of diversity, included a Christology that perceived Jesus as a holy messenger and exemplar rather than a savior who liberated through blood sacrifice. The Cathars' only prayer was the paternoster (Our Father) and their baptism (the *consolamentum*) was transmitted through the laying on of hands rather than through the medium of water. Furthermore, the Cathars saw themselves as true Christians hunted down by the "Church of Satan," which is how they referred to the Roman Catholic Church. The Perfects' purity, simplicity, and highly ethical behavior attracted increasing numbers of adherents and sympathizers, which included the aristocratic and wealthy. Eventually, the group's success constituted a direct challenge to Roman Catholic religious and political hegemony.[61]

When the Roman Catholic Church's preaching efforts failed to sway the French Cathars from their convictions, Pope Innocent III resorted to warfare. The "Albigensian Crusade" began in 1209.[62] Ostensibly, the sect's doctrinal heresy incited the attack on the Cathars. In truth, however, a complicated array of political and economic considerations fueled the campaign. The battle against the Cathars continued until 1256, when their last stronghold in France fell. During the decades of the conflict, tens of thousands of Cathars and their supporters died or were imprisoned. The Italian Catharist Church lasted somewhat longer, with the last Italian Perfect dying at the stake in 1321.[63] Legend has it that small enclaves of a covert Cathar tradition have survived to this day in the French countryside, although this is not easily verified.[64]

Scholars view Doinel's Gnostic Church as an example of neo-Catharism; however, some contemporary independent Catholic Gnostics find the term objectionable, preferring instead, "The Restoration of Gnosis."[65] As instructed by his séance contacts, Doinel formally established his church in 1890 and situated its liturgy and theology in Catharist doctrine and sacramental observances. Doinel penned numerous expositions on doctrine, including *La Gnose de Valentin* (The Valentinian Gnosis) and *Homilie Premiere* (The First Homily—"On the Holy Gnosis").[66]

Doinel's exposition on the complex and confounding

Valentinian cosmology begins with the first creation of the Absolute was Silence, the "unnamed, the ineffable, the abyss" [God]:

> Silence contained two "generators": male and female. These two are "the root and the source" of Being. The Absolute, as love, "contemplated itself with its eternal spouse, Ennoia (Thought) wished for an object of its love. The Abyss (the Absolute) through Ennoia, manifested the first two Aeons, Nous [Divine Intelligence—male] and Aletheia (Truth—female) simultaneously. (The "Absolute" brings forth these Aeons, "divine forces" in syzygies or pairs.) Next, Nous and Aletheia emanated two more Aeons, Logos and Zoe (Speech and Life), who in turn gave birth to Anthropos and Ecclesia. Many more Aeons are engendered similarly.
>
> Sophia was the very last Aeon created and thus the furthest from the Absolute. Subsequently, she felt great separation from the Absolute. To help Sophia, the Aeon Nous gave forth a new syzygy, Christ and Pneuma (Spirit). Sophia's great desire to be with the Absolute caused her to give birth to an Aeon called Achamoth (Terrestrial Sophia). She [Achamoth] was cast out of the Pleroma, but as she fell, she caught a glimpse of the "Ineffable Light that delighted her." Exiled into chaos, Achamoth was not allowed entrance into the Pleroma, which was guard-

ed by the Aeon Horos [Time]. She cried and her tears formed what we know as matter. Then the Aeon Horos, out of pity and concern for Achamoth, gave birth to the Aeon Jesus to be her companion. "Redeemed" by the influence of the Aeon Jesus, Achamoth "emanated three elements, the Pneumatic, the Psychic, and the Hylic." From these substances Achamoth created the Demiurge [Greek for "half-creator," who fashioned the material world], who Doinel calls the "unconscious worker of the worlds below." The Demiurge consisted both of Pleromic elements and "a natural element."

Satan is the Aeon of this world, birthed from matter, along with his minions, the perverse spirits. In order to oppose Satan, the Demiurge created Man but the Demiurge became jealous of Man because Achamoth imparted a "pneumatic [spiritual] seed" to him. Then Man disobeyed the Demiurge in the Garden of Eden and was cast out. In retaliation for this rebellion, the Demiurge caused Man to crave pleasures that veiled the "seed of light within him." Achamoth gave Grace to humans, to help them control "the base sexual desires."

Man is redeemed through the Aeon Jesus, who is not material, but "formed of a psychic principle borrowed from the Demiurge and an astral body." The Aeon Christ works through the Aeon Jesus—Christ gave Jesus "absolute power over Satan's world." Doinel describes three classes of human beings: the pneumatics, those elite humans who "follow the light of Achamoth;" the psychics, humans who exist somewhere between the realms of the Demiurge and of Achamoth; and the hylics, "subjects of Satan, whose soul is material and will be annihilated."[67]

While acting as patriarch under the name Tau Valentinus II, Doinel ordained both bishops and sophias (female bishops), including a central figure of the French occult revival, Dr. Gerard Encausse (Papus, 1865-1916), who assumed the spiritual name Tau Vincent, Bishop of Toulouse. Along with Papus, bishops Yvon LeLoup (a.k.a. Paul Sédir, 1871-1926) and Lucien Chamuel (Tau Bardesane, d. 1936) comprised the high synod of the church. In addition to his Masonic membership, Doinel joined Papus's Martinist Order in 1890 and eventually became a member of that society's Supreme Council. In 1892 Doinel consecrated several more bishops including Parisian luminaries like Symbolist poet Léonce-Eugène Fabre des Essarts (Tau Synésius, 1848-1917), physician and occult scholar Louis-Sophrone Fugairon (Tau Sophronius, b. 1848), and Marie Chauvel de Chauvignie (Esclarmonde, 1842-1927), the first female bishop in the Church.[68]

Doinel declared that his church was in direct line to John the Beloved, just as Fabré-Palaprat of *l'Église Johannites des Chrétiens Primitifs* had done over fifty years before. In 1893, the Holy Gnostic Synod declared that St. John's Gospel was the sole Gnostic Gospel. "Doinel's Gnostic Church combined the theological doctrines of

Simon Magus, Valentinus and Marcus (a later Valentinian noted for his development of the mysteries of numbers and letters and of the "mystic marriage") with sacraments derived from the Cathar Church and conferred in rituals that were heavily influenced by those of the Roman Catholic Church. At the same time, the Gnostic Church was intended to present a system of mystical Masonry."[69] From the outset, the Gnostic Church declared women and men to be absolute equals, ordaining both sexes to all clerical offices, and reflecting the Valentinian Gnostic philosophy. Fabre des Essarts addressed the issue of ordination of women: "Woman is the equal of Man, the indisputable *paredros* of the Anthropomorphic Syzygy, and as such she has the right to exercise the fullness of the priesthood and, by means of this, the vessel of infirmity, about which the Catholic Church speaks, becomes, for [or: within] Gnosis, the vessel of election!"[70]

Doinel based much of his sacramental practice on what he conceived of as historical Cathar theology and praxis as well as ancient Gnostic Christianity. Specifically, Doinel revived two historical Cathar sacraments, the *consolamentum* and the *appareillamentum* (spelled *apparellamentum* by various scholars).[71] Doinel also wrote a liturgy for a Gnostic Eucharist, *La fraction du Pain* (Breaking of the Bread).[72]

In Doinel's version of the *appareillamentum*, only a bishop or a Sophia may impart this sacrament of penance. After having petitioned for this sacrament, the penitent (who previously must have received the *consolamentum* at least once) met with the bishop at a pre-appointed time. This sacrament was only conferred in private. The supplicant, whose hands were bound with a white strip of cloth, knelt before the bishop and pled for pardon. The bishop then would lay his or her hands on the parishioner's head, offer words of comfort, and untie the binding cloth. The parishioner then recited the first verses of the Gospel of John and said, "God is love!"[73] The medieval Cathars' version of this sacrament "was a monthly rite, a collective confession of faults by the perfect, gathered for the ceremony presided over by a deacon or, on certain special occasions, the bishop."[74]

After leading the newly constituted church for a number of years, Doinel abdicated his patriarchate in the Gnostic Church in 1895 to the great shock of his followers and returned to the church of his youth, the Roman Catholic Church. Joining forces with Gabriel-Antoine Jogand-Pagès, a journalist and publisher who used the pen name Lèo Taxil, the two published denunciations of the Masons, the Gnostic Church, and Martinism, all organizations in which Doinel had previously been active. The former Gnostic patriarch even went so far as to publish a virulent anti-Masonic book entitled *Lucifer Démasqué* (Lucifer Unmasked) under the pseudonym "Jean Kostka." In 1897, a year after the publication of A. E. Waite's book debunking *Lucifer Démasqué*, Taxil revealed that his entire anti-Masonic campaign was an intricate hoax designed to embarrass the Roman Catholic Church.[75]

Fabre des Essarts, known in the church as Tau Synésius, assumed the patriarchate after Doinel's exodus. Under his leadership and with the assistance of Louis-Sophrone Fugairon, *l' Église Gnostique de France* gradually changed into "a Church of Christian Gnosis" instead of the explicitly Gnostic and Catharist church of Doinel. Fabre des

Essarts' newly fashioned church, *l'Église Chrétienne Moderne (néognostique)* supplanted Doinel's *l'Église Gnostique de France*. When Doinel recanted and wished to be reconciled to the Gnostic Church in 1900, it was in this church that Fabre des Essarts reconsecrated him as Tau Jules.[76]

Part Four: Jean Bricaud
and the *l'Église Catholique Gnostique*

In 1901, Fabre des Essarts consecrated twenty-year old Jean "Joanny" Bricaud (1881-1934) as Tau Johannes, Bishop of Lyon, an act that would effect major changes in the Church. In 1907, Bricaud left *l'Église Chrétienne Moderne (néognostique)* and with Papus and Fugairon formed a new church that the three bishops christened *l'Église Catholique Gnostique*. That same year the young bishop, who had been consecrated in the Johannine Church by Bishop Clément, was also made Patriarch of the Johannine Church (which was discussed in Part Two of this chapter).[77] Bricaud is a singular figure in Independent Catholic history because in his person three discrete lineages come together—the historic episcopate through Vilatte's line, Doinel's mystically appointed priesthood, and the earlier French esoteric churches, including *l'Église Johannites des Chrétiens Primitifs*.

Bricaud gave a homily on the occasion of his elevation to the patriarchal seat of *l'Église Catholique Gnostique*, which he also refers to as "the Holy Church of the Paraclete." Speaking to the gathered congregation, he preached that it was evident in the religious situation of the European people that Catholicism as it is taught and understood at this time does not meet the needs of modern society. Rather, it appears to most people as an oppressive force that dominates people by enslaving them in ignorance. In fact, he contended, if those religious people who dare to think of deserting the Church actually did so, it would portend the fall of Catholic orthodoxy. The Holy Church of the Paraclete, however, offers a new religion, that of Gnosticism. "Gnosis is the complete and final synthesis of all the beliefs and ideas that humanity needs to realize its origin, its past, its end, its nature, its future, the contradictions of existence and the problems of life.... Gnosis is the pearl of the Gospel for which humans really worthy of this name must sell all and give all to it." He further noted that "[B]y the term 'Christianity,' we do not understand it only to be the doctrines taught since the advent of the divine Saviour, but those taught before his arrival, in the ancient temples, the doctrines of Eternal Truth! Our Church is different from that of Rome. The name of that church is Force; the name of ours is Charity. Our Sovereign Patriarch is not Peter, the impulsive one who three times disavowed his Master...but John, the friend of the Saviour, the apostle that rested on Jesus' heart and knew Jesus most intimately, the oracle of light, the author of the eternal gospel...."[78]

From the episcopal pens of Bricaud and Fugairon came the *Profession de Foi* (Profession of Faith), which affirms twelve points of belief of the new church. Their tripartite theology departs quickly from the orthodox in describing the second member of the trinity: the Son, Jesus, whose person became inhabited by the divine word proclaimed by the [Aeon] *Christos* that came down [from the Pleroma]. This descent took place at Jesus' baptism and the *Christos* remained with Jesus until the moment of his passion. Through Jesus, the *Christos* instructed humans in gnosis and spiritual life, to deliver them from the slavery of the Demiurge and thus allow them to return to their original home, the pneumatic world.[79]

The founding of *l'Église Catholique Gnostique* marked a new era in French Gnosticism, one in which the Martinist tradition became inextricably woven into its fabric. Since Martinism and independent Gnostic churches became for all intents and purposes coterminous after 1907, it may be useful to look at the history and theology of Martinism, which is undertaken later in this chapter. Virtually all the French Gnostic bishops from 1907 until 1968 were also high initiates in Martinist lineages. It is difficult, therefore, to differentiate between Martinist philosophy and a discrete Gnostic Catholic theology since the two movements are so tightly interlaced. As shall be shown, the early French Gnostic churches eventually became an exoteric vehicle for those professing Martinism.

Part Five: The French State and the Roman Catholic Church, 1890-1920

While occult society thrived, the secular state and the Catholic church underwent great changes. In 1890, after almost a century of the concordatory Constitutional Church in France, Pope Leo XIII wished to improve relations with the French state. Rome's new conciliatory attitude towards the French government is known as the *raillement* (rallying) and was detailed in the papal encyclical, *Au milieu des sollicitudes*, which called for Catholics to work within the republican government for change.[80]

In the 1902 elections, "[t]he fate of the Church had

become the defining and only significant issue."[81] In the election aftermath, a former doctor and current radical politician named Émile Combes headed the new government. Formerly a candidate for the priesthood, Combes was a virulent anti-cleric as well as a Mason and spiritualist. When he initially took office, he tried to enforce a strict version of the Concordat, which resulted in the dissolution of religious orders and the destruction of the Catholic schools. Under Combes' direction, "Two hundred thousand members of 3,216 orders were banned, including the main teaching order in boys' schools (the *Frères des Écoles Chrétiennes*), and innumerable female orders that provided most of the country's child care, female education, medical care, and welfare. A third of Catholic schools were shut. It was an act of social vandalism by men who did not have to bear the consequences."[82] In response to Combes' draconian measures, Rome cut off diplomatic relations with France in 1904. Forced into a corner, Combes relented and abolished the Concordat.[83] On December 9, 1905, the French government passed legislation that separated church and state. Even though this separation cost the Church many millions of francs in state support, "in the long run, separation was arguably positive because the church was freed from state control and created its own lay organizations."[84]

Fin de siècle France saw increased attacks on Catholic hegemony by *libre-pensée* [free thought] societies that had begun to be established in 1848. Initially founded to offer a secular alternative to religious funerals, more than 1,000 societies existed around the turn of the century. One way in which citizens chose to thumb their nose at the Church was to mandate for themselves a non-religious funeral and a tombstone engraved with secular sentiments. In the estimation of these *libre-pensée*, Christianity was an impediment to scientific progress and moreover was "anti-social" because of its dogmatic emphasis on personal soteriology. "Day-to-day *libre-pensée* activity consisted of minor insults to Catholic susceptibilities, eating sausages at Good Friday banquets, mocking Christian dogma...campaigning to 'de-baptise' street names and ban Catholic processions."[85]

Amid this increasingly anti-Roman Catholic atmosphere, Archbishop Joseph René Vilatte returned to France in 1907. In Anson's opinion, "The anti-clerical government of the nineteen hundreds was only too ready to encourage any project to set up a National Church in France independent of the Holy See."[86] Encouraged by the French secular government, Vilatte established an Old Catholic Gallican church, *l'Église Catholique Apostolique Française* in 1907 and then departed the country later that same year. Julien-Ernest Houssaye took over as primate of *l'Église Catholique Apostolique Française* from Vilatte in 1907. Houssaye, known as Abbé Julio, was a former Roman Catholic priest who had been raised to the episcopate in 1904 by Paolo Miraglia-Gulotti (who Vilatte had consecrated in 1900 in Italy).[87] Under Houssaye, the church focused increasingly on magic and occultism. Fascinated by magic and healing through the power of prayer and the Mass, Houssaye wrote numerous books along these lines, including, *Prières Merveilleuses* (1896), *Prières Liturgiques (1900), Prières Liturgiques Tome II: calendrier perpetuel, invocation des saints, neuvaines, saints patrons* (1908), *Le Livre Secret des Grandes Exorcisms et*

Benedictions (1902), and *Grands secrets merveilleux* (1906).[88]

French monk Louis-Marie-Francois Giraud (1876-1950) left his Cisterican monastery and joined *l'Église Catholique Apostolique Française,* receiving ordination to the priesthood from Vilatte on 21 June 1907. Houssaye consecrated Giraud as bishop (who was likewise inclined to the study of magic) on 21 June 1911, at a ceremony near Geneva. Giraud settled in the French town of Gazinet, near Bordeaux, which became the center of his ministry. The Vilatte-Giraud lineage is important to delineate because Doinel's Gnostic Church becomes legitimized through this line, as least as far as the issue of historical apostolic succession is concerned. Jean Bricaud, a former Roman Catholic seminarian who became a major figure in French Gnostic circles, may have been ordained in 1912 by Giraud; Giraud definitely consecrated Bricaud on 13 July 1913.[89]

Part Six: Martinez de Pasqually and the *Élus Cohen*

As indicated earlier, the history of Martinism is intimately related to the French Gnostic church lineages. Serge Caillet, a French Martinist and scholar of the tradition, defines the word to denote the doctrine and theurgical practices of Martinez de Pasqually (c.1709-1774),[90] as well as the theosophy[91] of Louis-Claude de Saint-Martin (1743-1803). It also may refer to Jean-Baptiste Willermoz's Rectified Scottish Rite, a Masonic system that he established after the death of his teacher, Pasqually. Additionally, the term is used to refer to the distinct Martinist Order that Dr. Gèrard Encausse founded in the late 1800s and its filial descendents, as well as to those who follow Saint-Martin's teachings, whether or not they belong to an established Martinist order. Martinez de Pasqually's Masonic organization became one of the most prominent esoteric societies to emerge at this time; his students, Louis-Claude de Saint-Martin and Jean-Baptiste Willermoz (1730-1824), continued to advance his legacy in their separate and distinctive ways. In the modern era, two primary currents of the tradition exist, according to Caillet: the Papusian lineage, and the Ambelain lineage of the "neo-Cohens," both which will be discussed later in this chapter.[92]

Modern Martinists look to Martinez de Pasqually as the seminal inspiration of their essential doctrine. Very little documentation exists about Pasqually's early life other than the fact that he spent a decade in the Spanish military as a young man. The son of a Freemason, Pasqually was also an enthusiastic Mason, and in 1754 founded a Masonic lodge in Montpellier. In 1762, he established a lodge in Bordeaux called the *Temple des Élus Cohen* (Temple of the Elect Cohens), which a young Saint-Martin joined. Eventually he set up his own version of Masonry, the *Ordre de Chevaliers Maçons Élus Coens de L'Univers*. It was into this order that Pasqually initiated Jean-Baptiste Willermoz, a critical figure in Masonic history. Pasqually spent the years from 1767-1772 systematizing his teachings and writing rituals that he distributed to his students. In 1771, Saint-Martin began helping him with this task.[93]

Kabbalistic elements, including number mysticism (gematria), figure prominently in Pasqually's complex cosmology. He outlined his tenets in his only book, *Traité sur la réintégration des êtres dans leur première propriété, vertu et puissance spirituelle divine* (*Treatise on the Reintegration of*

Beings into their own virtues, powers and qualities), a volume considered a modern theosophical tour de force.[94] The mythos underlying Pasqually's concepts is based on a kabbalistic interpretation of portions of the Bible, primarily Genesis. Briefly outlined, humans are essentially divine in nature and potentiality, and are ranked above the angelic order in the original scheme of creation; God charged them to administer a peaceful, orderly universe and restrict the wicked. The angelic order, on the other hand, was created to praise Him and to relish a divine life; they did not have the elevated administrative responsibilities conferred upon humankind.

Then the plan went awry. The disobedient angels or "perverse beings," as Pasqually calls them, rebelled, resolving to exist in opposition to God. Subsequently, these insubordinate angels seduced humans into their nefarious design. Robert Ambelain, a Martinist and French Gnostic bishop, describes the scenario: "Under the impulse of the perverse beings, Archetypal Man made himself an independent demiurge, thereby breaking the very laws he was ordained to observe. He dared to make himself a creator [creating the material world] in turn and to be equal to God by his deeds." He delineates the agenda of the evil angels: they have taken shelter in the material world in order to separate themselves further from God. Their plan is to keep humans captive, in order that humans might "organize and animate" the earth, rather like indentured servants. As he expresses it: "To escape the cycles of reincarnation in this infernal world, man must detach himself from everything that attracts him to matter.... The fallen entities, however, constantly fight man's tendency towards perfection by tempting him constantly so as to make him stay in world where they can maintain their rulership over him."[95]

In order to break free from the material illusion and their enslavement to the perverse beings that hold them in a hypnotic sway, humans must employ their will, which is the only divine faculty they have retained in their dissipated state. God sent the Repairer (Jesus Christ),[96] to illuminate the path to restoration of humankind's true place in the cosmos. If humans realize that they possess amazing celestial potentialities and powers, they will be in a position to release themselves from their exile in the material world. Regaining the Adamic legacy that was abandoned in the Fall, they can resume their rightful cosmological standing. Once this is achieved, humans become dedicated to the reintegration of all beings, including the natural world, helping them return to their divinely ordained roles and conditions.

Pasqually held that the practice of a complex system of ceremonial magic was an important element in spiritual advancement.[97] He considered one of the consequences of the Fall to have been a cessation of communication between humans and the Divine. Theurgic operations were needed, therefore, in order to contact intermediaries who would connect the ritualist with Christ. On the surface, there seems to be a discrepancy in the fact that the Roman Catholic Church prohibited its congregants from Masonic involvement and the vast majority of Élus Cohen, including Pasqually himself, and later Saint-Martin, were practicing Roman Catholics. McIntosh clarifies the curious situation; although Clement XII had issued a papal bull opposing Freemasonry in 1738, it was for the most part disregarded in France. Roman Catholic laity and even priests were active in the French Freemasonry movement. Freemasonry enjoyed a huge degree of popularity in predominately Roman Catholic France during the latter eighteenth century.[98]

In 1772, at the height of the Élus Cohen's popularity, Pasqually sailed to San Domingo to oversee some family matters. He never returned to France, dying in Port-au-Prince, Haiti, on 20 September 1774. By 1778, most of the Élus Cohen temples were shuttered, although at least two carried on until the Revolution.[99]

According to Serge Caillet, Robert Ambelain (Sar[100] Aurifer, 1907-1997) "reawakened" the Élus Cohen in 1942-43 during the Nazi occupation of France, even in the face of German persecution of Masonic societies. Ambelain's newly constituted "Martinist Order of the Élus Cohen" was dedicated to the theurgic rites of Pasqually. Caillet believes that although there was no direct ritual initiatic succession between Pasqually and Ambelain, there was a valid "spiritual filiation."[101] After operating for several years, Ambelain put the lodge to rest, only to revive it thirty years later. Orders still exist that call themselves Élus Cohen and claim to be spiritual heirs to Pasqually's ceremonial magic system.

Part Seven: Louis-Claude de Saint-Martin and Jean-Baptiste Willermoz

In the years immediately preceding the French Revolution, France's fragile economic, social, and political state of affairs fostered the exponential growth of that country's esoteric, spiritualistic, and occult groups. It was at this time that the man Antoine Faivre lauds as "the most important Christian esotericist of his time, whose influence, directly or indirectly, has never ceased to spread." Faivre is referring to Louis-Claude de Saint-Martin, Pasqually's foremost disciple.[102]

Saint-Martin was born in France in 1743 and as a young man, he joined the military. While he was stationed at Bordeaux, he encountered Pasqually, who initiated him into the Élus Cohen in 1768. From 1768-1771, Pasqually employed Saint-Martin as his personal secretary and in 1771 Saint-Martin left the military to give over his life to spiritual study.[103] Even previous to the death of Pasqually in 1774, however, Saint-Martin slowly began to move away from his master's emphasis on theurgy.[104]

Saint-Martin believed, in line with Pasqually's philosophy, that human beings were of supreme importance in the divine plan. They possessed godlike abilities and were Christs *in potentio*, but most frittered away their lives as sleepwalkers, unaware of the latent powers within. To become reborn is a difficult path, Saint-Martin acknowledged, and he saw self-discipline and to some degree asceticism as essential aspects of the inner way. He advocated that humankind recover its primeval nature and supremacy through the regenerative influence of Christ, through spiritual contemplation and prayer, through the exercise of will and devotion to God; success in this endeavor results in a second birth, a creation of the "New Man."

In 1775 Saint-Martin published his first book, *Des Erreurs et de la Vérité, par un Philosophe Inconnu* (*Of Errors and the Truth, by an Unknown Philosopher*), which the Spanish Inquisition condemned in 1798. Always writing under the moniker, "the Unknown Philosopher," he followed this tome with several more books in which he "sought to combat modern rationalist and materialist reductionism."[105] By 1803, when Saint-Martin died of a stroke, his works had circulated throughout France and in many other European countries as well, garnering him a notable reputation as a philosopher.

A member of the original Élus Cohen tribunal and a close friend of Saint-Martin, Jean-Baptiste Willermoz directed the vibrant Élus Cohen temple in Lyons. After Pasqually's death, Willermoz became a central figure in the reformation of French Templar Masonry. In 1778, satisfied that he had discovered the esoteric secrets of Masonry, he founded a Masonic order that taught inner Christian teachings in the higher degrees.[106] Willermoz called his society the "Rectified Scottish Rite," which included the degree of *l'Ordre des Chevaliers Bienfaisants de la Cité Sainte* (Order of the Knights Beneficent of the Holy City). Willermoz presupposed a link to the medieval Order of the Knights Templar, considered by him to be one of the repositories of ancient and divinely inspired wisdom, transmitted through lodge initiates to the present day.[107]

Part Eight: Modern Martinism

The era of modern Martinism commenced during the period of the occult revival in France. Dr. Gèrard Encausse (1865-1916), whose magical and pen name was Papus, was initiated into Martinism in 1882[108] and founded a Martinist order in 1891. While he was baptized and confirmed a Roman Catholic, Papus would eventually be considered a "serious adversary" of the Church.[109] He was a member of the Paris temple of the Hermetic Order of the Golden Dawn as well as the Kabbalistic

Order of the Rose-Croix under Grand Master Marquis Stanislaus de Guaita. *L'Ordre Martiniste* (The Martinist Order), whose official name was *L'Ordre des Supèrieurs Inconnus* (Order of the Unknown Superiors), initially consisted of a twelve-member supreme council with Papus as Grand Master and President.[110] Other original members of the tribunal included occultists Josephin Péladan (1858-1918) and Stanislaus de Guaita (1861-1897), cofounders of the Kabbalistic Order of the Rose-Croix.[111] As the order grew, it attracted numerous occultists and visionaries, including René Guénon (1886-1951), who was affiliated with the Martinist Order between 1906 and 1912.[112]

Papus wished to create a society that would bring together Martinist initiates and provide an opportunity for further study and promulgation of the Martinist teachings.[113] His Martinist Order flourished in the next quarter of a century, spreading as far as Russia and the court of Nicholas II.[114] The Martinist Order under Papus was officially allied with an independent sacramental church, the *l'Église Gnostique Universelle* (The Universal Gnostic Church—UGC), whose origins were in Jules Doinel's afore-mentioned *l'Église Gnostique de France*. In February 1908, the newly established episcopal synod elected Jean Bricaud (1882-1934), who took the name Tau Jean II, as the new church's patriarch. The church headed by Bricaud changed its name to *l'Église Gnostique Universelle* (EGU). To avoid confusion with Bricaud's group, Fabre des Essarts' church became identified as *l'Église Gnostique de France*.

Between 1910 and 1916, Bricaud and Papus corresponded about the issue of an esoteric church. Papus was searching for an exoteric structure with which to link the Martinist Order and to this end he sought affiliations with small churches such as the EGU. Even after the 1911 treaty officially designating the EGU as the official Martinist church, confusion and arguments about the designation still flew. Bricaud explained to Papus that the exoteric Roman Catholic Church had the Pope as its head; for the esoteric church, there was the Gnostic Patriarch. Bricaud and Papus evidently came to an understanding because the Martinist Order reaffirmed this affiliation in 1918.[115] In 1913, Louis-Marie-François Giraud consecrated Bricaud, thus legitimizing the EGU in terms of traditional apostolic succession, which came through Giraud from the Vilatte lineage. In 1916, Papus died while serving as a French army surgeon and caring for soldiers at the front. After his demise, his renewed Martinist movement lost its unity and began to fragment with the loss of its unfaltering guide. The structure of the Martinist world became increasingly complicated, as orders splintered and formed new alliances and orders.[116]

Martinism is still a vital part of the esoteric subculture, although the actual number of adherents does not seem to be large. Caillet reflects: "By definition, initiatic schools are reserved for a small number of people.... Therefore, we must not be surprised to see that this number is relatively low, even though the research being done by various [Martinist] groups has intensified at the end of the 20th century and the beginning of the 21st. Initiatic paths are closed paths and narrow paths."[117]

Although from the time of Papus at least until 1968, many Martinist luminaries, including Jules Doinel, René Guénon, Papus, Jean Bricaud, Victor Blanchard, Constant

Chevillon, Robert Ambelain, and Phillippe Encausse (Papus' son, 1906-1984), held clerical offices in independent sacramental Gnostic churches, most of the larger Martinist orders are no longer officially aligned with specific churches or ecclesiastical bodies. There seems to be little direct influence of the Martinist movement on contemporary independent esoteric sacramental churches, although individual IESC members often belong to one or more occult or esoteric orders. In that sense, there is some continued overlap and cross-fertilization between Martinism and the independent sacramental movement.[118]

Chapter Three
Arnold Harris Mathew and the
Early History of the Liberal Catholic Church

Part One: Arnold Harris Mathew

Arnold Harris Mathew (1852–1919), the first British Old Catholic bishop, underwent a strange ecclesiastical journey rivaling the convoluted life of Joseph René Vilatte, although Mathew limited his adventuring to the geographical confines of Western Europe. Before we examine his singular biography it would be helpful to briefly explore the religious milieu of mid- and late-Victorian England, the initial setting of this chapter's history. Especially illuminating is an understanding of the Anglo-Catholic revival and the debate around the validity of Anglican holy orders.

In the foreword to Brandreth's classic *Episcopi Vagantes and the Anglican Church*, Rev. Canon J.A. Douglas tries to comprehend the enormous increase of *episcopi vagantes*[1] in England and America from about 1850 to 1950. According to Douglas, the phenomenon of irregular bishops was almost unheard of in the Middle Ages and he knows of none in the seventeenth and eighteenth centuries. He notes that until the Tractarian movement and the Anglo-Catholic revival in the mid-1800s, most probably the only people concerned with the validity of Anglican orders were theologians. By the 1890s, though, valid apostolic orders became a general topic of concern in the Anglican Church. Writing in 1947, Douglas maintains that the Anglo-Catholic revival and the subsequent questions about the validity of orders provided the impetus for this proliferation of *episcopi vagantes*.[2]

The Tractarian movement (also called the Oxford movement) and the various streams of Anglo-Catholicism of the high Victorian period rocked the Church of England; at the time an immense and heterogeneous institution that David Morse notes wryly was a "massive force for inertia."[3] The High Church Victorian revival was related in certain ways to the seventeenth-century High Church theologians, including Richard Hooker (1554-1645), Richard Bancroft (1544-1610), and the Caroline Divines.[4] Generally speaking, the High Church tradition emphasizes the primacy of the apostolic succession, the Catholicism of the Church, and a high doctrine of the Church in which the State is "aware of its divinely ordained function as the protector of the Church."[5] While the Tractarian movement of 1833-1848 is often conflated with High Church theology and Anglo-Catholicism, there exists subtle but important differences between these groups. Even within Anglo-Catholicism, which has as its raison d'être to catholicize the Anglican Church, there exists great diversity. Pickering contends that while the Tractarians and Anglo-Catholics have similar objectives, namely to restore and revivify the Catholic nature of the Anglican Church, the Anglo-Catholics advocated a much more rapid pace of change within nineteenth-century Church life. The Tractarians, on the other hand, advocated a more measured and gradual Catholic restoration firmly grounded in the traditional Anglican Book of Common Prayer.

At the height of the Anglo-Catholic movement in the 1920s and 1930s, some Anglo-Catholic clergy traveled to Italy and France and returned with quantities of Roman Catholic vestments and accoutrements such as confessionals, ciboria, and monstrances. Along with such paraphernalia, these clergy instituted devotions such as the exposition of the Blessed Sacrament, the chanting of the rosary, and prayers to the Saints and the Holy Mother.[6] Devotion to the Saints including the Blessed Virgin was not a part of the Tractarian platform, as they considered it against Anglican tradition in light of the 1662 Prayer Book. There were, however, points of accord between the two movements including an emphasis on the inherently catholic nature of the Anglican Church, stress on the Incarnation rather than the Protestant emphasis on atonement, the centrality of the sacraments (especially the Eucharist), the reinstitution of nuns and monks, and "auricular" confession.[7]

The popularity of Anglo-Catholicism, which was due in part to its simple and straightforward formula of religiosity for the laity, is demonstrated by the rise in membership of the Anglo-Catholic society, the English Church Union. Founded in 1860, it began with 200 members. By 1894, membership had grown to 35,000 and by 1901, to 39,000.[8]

The Tractarian movement was an assemblage of Oxford fellows who were highly dissatisfied with the increasing liberalism of Anglican Church. Archconservatives in a political and social sense, they argued against a laxity of doctrine, erastianism (subverting the Church's traditional power to the state) and disestablishment.[9] For the Tractarians, the Church was divinely constituted and of divine status. Issues of authority were at the heart of the debates that rankled the nineteenth-century Church of England, including "the authority of the Church as an autonomous body over against the state; the limits of the state's authority within a church still recognized as the church of the nation; the nature of the authority to be ascribed to the sources of the Church's teaching—the Scriptures, the Fathers of the Church, and the Prayer Book."[10]

Since the eighteenth century, the Church had been accused of clerical abuses of power including simony and "the holding of multiple livings."[11] Politicians and Anglican clergy of the 1820s and 1830s campaigned vociferously for reforms within the Church, and those two decades saw legislative activity aimed at lessening church corruption and increasing suffrage. Most notably, the repeal of the Test and Corporation Acts in 1828 and passing of the Catholic Emancipation Act in 1829 increased general civil rights for Dissenters and Roman Catholics, while the Reform Act of 1832 initiated much needed electoral reform. In 1832, the Whig government formed the Ecclesiastical Committee in order to examine the activities of the Church and to suggest improvements. The Tractarians saw these political acts as intolerable interferences by the State into the divinely sanctioned institution of the Church.[12] As Owen Chadwick writes, "It is safe to say that the [Tractarian] Movement would not have taken the form which it took without the impetus of ecclesiastical and secular politics."[13] The final straw for the Tractarians was the Whig government's Irish Church Temporalities Bill, which aimed to reduce the number of bishoprics in Ireland and funnel the money elsewhere. This bill occasioned Rev. John Keble's fervent Assize Sermon of 1833, entitled "National Apostasy," which condemned state interference with the Church of England and is seen as the beginning of the Oxford movement.[14]

After that rousing oration, the founding members of the Oxford movement—John Henry Newman, John Keble, and Edward Pusey—began publishing tracts outlining their views. At that time, Oxford University was an Anglican institution and its fellows were priests who stayed unmarried as long as they held their fellowships. Since specialized schools of divinity were unheard of in England during that period, British clergy as well as future leaders of Church and State were educated primarily at Oxford and Cambridge.[15]

In addition to the divine status of the Church, the Tractarian's central concerns revolved around the Real Presence in the Eucharist and the subject of apostolic succession. For definitive positions on these matters, the Oxford movement looked back to the Church Fathers as the arbiters of the original and undefiled form of Christianity. The considerable accumulation of patristic scholarship from the sixteenth-century onward, as a consequence of the "New Learning," had a salutary effect on the efforts of Tractarians. The inauguration of the "New Learning" was due to the fall of Constantinople in 1453 and the subsequent exiling of Byzantine scholars to Italy, which had reintroduced Europe to the classical Greek philosophers. The resultant gains in research revealed early Christianity in a vastly different light than had previously been supposed.[16] As better editions of the patristic works were printed and critical research and linguistic methods employed, it was clear that the patristic writers favored the traditionalists rather than the reformers. This new knowledge unveiled the church fathers, for the most part, as endorsing the centrality of the bishop to church polity, a high regard for the celibate life, auricular confession, and even devotions to the Saints and the Blessed Virgin, as well as a deep sense of the sacredness of the world. "In short...the advance of patristic scholarship befriended the conservative and traditional element everywhere in Protestantism; and nowhere more significantly than in the Church of England."[17]

In 1839, Newman started an in-depth study of the Donatist and Monophysite heresies of the early Church. His intense research only deepened his questions in regard to the Anglican position on the primacy of the pope, the nature of apostolic succession, and the necessity of church union. After much contemplation, Newman submitted to Rome in October 1845, an act that engendered feelings of shock and betrayal among his fellow Tractarians.[18] His reception into the Roman Catholic Church gave rise to the charge that the forgone conclusion of the Oxford movement was ultimately conversion. While his decision drew great criticism and anger from many Anglo-Catholics, others followed his example, leading one scholar to exclaim: "The carnage in the Church of England was frightful."[19] Although many of those Anglo-

Catholics who remained in the English church prayed for a reunion with Rome, those hopes were dashed when the Vatican officially denied the validity of Anglican orders in 1896.

Arnold Harris Mathew, the British Old Catholic bishop who eventually became caught up in the validity debate, was born in France in 1852, just seven years after Newman's conversion. The child of a French mother and an English father, his first baptism was at the hands of a French Catholic abbé; he later underwent baptism by an Anglican priest. As he grew up, he attended rites in both the Roman Catholic Church and Church of England.[20] For most of his life, he vacillated between Canterbury and Rome, an ambiguity undoubtedly precipitated by his baptism and upbringing in two different church bodies.

Mathew commenced his lifelong clerical vocation at age of 25, when he was ordained a Roman Catholic priest in Glasgow. Between 1879 and 1889, he served in several dioceses, never staying long in one area. In May 1889 he resigned his priestly orders after suffering a crisis of faith. That same year Rome placed him under the lesser excommunication.[21]

Between 1889 and 1890, there was general surprise when Mathew became a member of the Unitarian Church, a dramatic volte-face from Catholicism. The denomination's primary newspaper, *The Inquirer*, published a laudatory article in its 12 July 1889 issue, celebrating Mathew's enrollment. The Unitarian fold did not contain him for long—hardly more than one year—before he turned to the Anglican Church for spiritual sustenance and employment. The Bishop of London, Dr. Temple, allowed Mathew to officiate at weddings at the Anglo-Catholic

Holy Trinity Church, Sloane Street, which was irregular considering that he was not an Anglican.[22] In addition, Church of England authorities invited him to work in one of their congregations on an unofficial basis, under Canon Robert Eyton. The experiment was a failure; Mathew found the Canon odious and "lewd."[23] (Rev. Eyton eventually left England amid charges of serious albeit unspecified immorality.[24])

Realizing that he was not suited to serve within "the Establishment," as he put it, Mathew relinquished his post under Eyton in 1892 and retired from the ministry until 1907. He never officially re-joined or took orders in the Church of England although he was married in an Anglican Church in 1892. One barrier to his formal enrollment was his adamant refusal to sign the "Form of Renunciation of Roman Errors." He did, however, engage in correspondence with the Archbishop of Canterbury in 1907, inquiring about a ministerial position in the Church, although this proposal never fructified.[25]

In 1907 Rev. Richard O'Halloran contacted Mathew and encouraged him to enter the clerical arena once more. O'Halloran, a suspended Roman Catholic priest in charge of a fledgling mission in the west London community of Ealing, wished to establish an Old Catholic church in England. He had already unsuccessfully approached an Old Catholic bishop for consecration in 1902. Five years later, still hoping and enthusiastic to bring the Old Catholic church to Britain, O'Halloran prevailed upon Mathew to consider consecration in the Old Catholic Church. The priest informed him that there was a great need for such a church and that a synod in Chelsfield, Hertfordshire, had elected Mathew to the bishopric. Hearing this, Mathew agreed to the arrangement.[26]

Archbishop Gerald Gul, assisted by three other Old Catholic bishops, consecrated Mathew at St. Gertrude's Cathedral in Utrecht on 28 April 1908. The ceremony, originally scheduled for April 8, had to be postponed when the Old Catholic bishops, to their great astonishment, found out that Mathew was married and the father of three children. Although no married priest had yet been raised to the episcopate in the Old Catholic Church, the bishops eventually gave their permission for Mathew's consecration to proceed. Ultimately it was revealed that there existed little interest among the English for such a church but purportedly Mathew did not find that out until after his consecration. As James Wedgwood put it, "the number of active adherents in that country could be counted on one hand."[27]

In a letter to the Archbishop of Canterbury in May 1909, Mathew referred to this situation, writing, "I neither desired nor sought...Episcopal Consecration. I was completely deceived and entirely misled by _____,[28] a man who has deceived many besides myself...." Mathew claimed that once he realized that there was, in fact, no Old Catholic congregation in England, he offered to resign, saying that a particular priest (O'Halloran) had made "certain statistical representations" about parishioners to the Old Catholic bishops that were untrue.[29] The Old Catholic bishops declined his offer of resignation and instead affirmed their confidence in Mathew.

Now active as a bishop in Britain, Mathew first ordained Rev. Noel Lambert, a Congregationalist minister, in 1909, and followed this with other ordinations and the establishment of a "cathedral." Like his other ecclesial affiliations, Mathew's connection with the Old Catholics proved to be short-lived. He was in full communion with the Old Catholics until 29 December 1910, when he made his separation formal in a document entitled, "Declaration of Autonomy and Independence."[30] The Old Catholic conference of bishops officially withdrew their recognition of Bishop Mathew in 1913.[31]

Nonetheless his episcopal activities did not slow down at all after cutting ties with the Old Catholics. In 1911 he consecrated four of his eight priests as bishops; the new bishops in turn elected him "Archbishop of London." Once the Vatican was informed of these goings-on, Mathew was placed under the greater excommunication.[32] In the declaration of excommunication, dated 11 February, 1911, Pope Pius X charged that Mathew was a "pseudo-bishop" who "has not hesitated to arrogate unto himself the title of 'Anglo-Catholic Archbishop of London.'"[33] Two years later, Mathew unsuccessfully sued the *Times* of London for libel after the paper published an excerpt of the papal document excommunicating him.[34]

During this period, Mathew consecrated two bishops that proved especially important to the future of the independent sacramental movement: Prince de Landas Berghes[35] and Frederick Samuel Willoughby.[36] Prince de Landas Berghes (1873-1920), a Roman Catholic and a member of the Austrian royal family born in Italy, became friends with Mathew, who ordained the prince in 1912 and consecrated him in 1913. Due to the outbreak of the Great War in August 1914, de Landas Berghes was in jeopardy of being interred as an enemy alien. The British Foreign Office, aware that he was related to numerous European royal families, arranged passage for him to the United States in 1914. Once in America, Bishop de

Landas Berghes consecrated several bishops who became important leaders in the Old Catholic movement in America, including Carmel Henry Carfora in 1916 and Stanislaus Mickiewicz in 1917. Before his death, Bishop de Landas Berghes returned to the Roman Catholic fold. He died in an Augustinian community in Pennsylvania in 1920.[37]

Although Frederick Samuel Willoughby (1862-1928) confined his brief Old Catholic ministry to the United Kingdom, his lineal descendants established the Liberal Catholic Church, which became the most numerically successful of all the Mathew successions.[38] The beginning of the LCC goes back to 1913, when the young James Ingall Wedgwood (1892-1951), a scion of the famous china manufacturing dynasty and an ardent Theosophist, became a member of Mathew's small congregation and was ordained soon after his entrance. Willoughby, formerly an Anglo-Catholic priest, joined Mathews in 1914 and in short order was ordained as well. When de Landas Berghes departed the country, Mathew was left without a coadjucator bishop with whom to run the diocese. Not long after the prince's exodus, therefore, Mathew informed his congregation that an election had been held, resulting in Willoughby being elected to the bishopric over Wedgwood. Willoughby's consecration was held in October 1914, witnessed by two canons, both of whom belonged to the Theosophical Society and the Order of the Star in the East, the society founded in 1911 to prepare for the advent of a World-Teacher in the person of Jiddu Krishnamurti.[39]

By this time, more Theosophists had joined the congregation. What drew these esotericists into the conservative bastion of Mathew's church? While there is not enough information to say for sure, one may surmise that the traditional Catholic ritual, including the liturgy, vestments, and other paraphernalia, may have been highly attractive to Wedgwood and Willoughby, both former Anglo-Catholics, along with other Theosophists. Old Catholicism also offered a method of being Catholic but not Roman, with the added inducement of a claim to apostolic succession. Since Leo XIII formally condemned Anglican orders in his bull *Apostolicae Curae* in 1896, those Theosophists wishing to become priests in the apostolic line may have felt more secure with orders originating from the independent Dutch Catholic lineage. As part of joining Mathew's Ancient Catholic Church of Great Britain, Wedgwood signed a statement averring that he was 'formally united with the Ancient (Catholic) Church of England, Scotland, and Ireland' and professed his belief in 'the Decrees of the Seven Holy Ecumenical councils as laid down, in precise terms, in the Niceno-Constantinopolitan Creed of the Universal Church, the Dogma of Transubstantiation, the Seven Sacraments, and the Decrees of the Synod of Jerusalem 1672."[40] In light of Madame Blavatsky's negative views of traditional Christianity and specifically the apostolic succession, though, it seems a curious move for her followers to adhere themselves to an orthodox church. The democratization of spirituality as advocated initially by Theosophy campaigned against the idea of a priesthood to "mediate" between the individual soul and the Atman.[41] The tension caused by Christian-oriented factions within the Theosophical Society will be probed later in this chapter.

One must ask why Mathew accepted the Theosophists

into his fold, since at this time, the prelate held a highly orthodox stance on doctrine. Given Mathew's highly erratic nature, though, it was not out of character for Mathew to act in ways that defy logical explanation. For whatever reason, Mathew denounced the Theosophical Society in a letter to his congregants dated 6 August 1915, declaring that no one could be both a member of his church and a Theosophist or a member of the Order of the Star in the East. In response to this ultimatum, Willoughby, Wedgwood, and most of Mathew's parishioners left to form a separate Old Catholic Church. A more detailed account of the origins and early history of the LCC will be related later in this chapter.[42]

Also in 1915, Mathew penned a missive to the Archbishop of Canterbury with his idea of founding an offshoot of the Old Catholic Church in Britain. The Archbishop of Canterbury's secretary wrote back that it seemed to be Mathew's goal to invite the Bishop of London to be reconsecrated by Mathew. In addition, the secretary continued, Mathew appeared to be asking that the Church of England recognize him and his congregation as "representatives of the Holy Catholic Church in this country."[43] The Archbishop of Canterbury himself wrote, "...believing as I do that the Church of England is in this country the true representative of the Catholic Church as it comes down to us from the past, I can hardly be expected to look favourably upon the establishment in England of another society claiming that position."[44]

In another communiqué, Mathew tried to clear up any misunderstanding but most likely only offended the Archbishop in even greater measure: "We are not so absurd as to claim to be, exclusively, 'The Holy Catholic

Church in this country'! but rather...[a] very humble little Catholic *Mission*, possessing indisputable orders and valid sacraments." Mathew took this opportunity to point out that the Roman Church did not recognize the Church of England's orders as valid; Pope Leo XIII had declared them "absolutely null and utterly void." If the Bishop of London were reconsecrated, then his orders would be "negotiable" all around the world, in Mathew's opinion. Needless to say, the Anglicans ignored his bumbling entreaties. The Archbishop of Canterbury went so far as to have a statement outlining Mathew's history published in the *Guardian* on 19 August, 1915. Mathew complained to the Archbishop that his private letters to the prelate were treated carelessly and in this way the Archbishop helped his "persecutors."[45]

After this series of debacles, Mathew, left with very few congregants and no priests, publicly resigned his bishopric in January 1916 and planned to re-enter the Roman Catholic Church. The terms of submission to Rome proved not to his liking, however, and later that year he restarted his Old Catholic mission, under the rubric of "The Western Uniate Catholic Church."[46] This jurisdiction is the origin of another independent Catholic lineage resulting from Mathew's consecration of Bernard Mary Williams to the episcopate on 14 April 1914. In 1917, Mathew chose Williams as his coadjucator and successor, and Williams remained one of his few loyal supporters until the end of Mathew's life.[47]

Mathew once again approached the long-suffering Archbishop of Canterbury for a clerical position but was refused, although the Archbishop did consent to allow him to join the Church as a member of the laity. Mathew declined the offer. He lived his remaining few years in poverty with few friends, supporters or family members, his wife having divorced him long before. Mathew died in December 1919 and was buried with Anglican rites.[48]

Part Two: The British Occult Revival and the Origins of the Liberal Catholic Church

Understanding mid- and late-Victorian religious sensibilities as well as the Edwardian cultural and intellectual milieu lends a useful context in which to locate the Liberal Catholic Church (LCC), founded in England in 1916. In the mid-Victorian age, the social and cultural fabric of England was being undone and rewoven in new ways, as increased urbanization and mechanization changed the nature of domicile and work for many. Amazing inventions such as the modern steam locomotive (1830), the telegraph (c. 1844), and the telephone (1876) meant people could travel and communicate faster and farther than ever before. The magical qualities of such fabrications indicated to some Victorians that the world was imbued with mysterious, intangible, and often unsettling, energies.[49]

This increasingly automated fast-paced society may have been at the root of much of Victorian anxiety and sense of alienation. Historians theorize that in the mid-1850s and onward, developments in science and the progressively more impersonal social order sparked the oft-mentioned "Victorian crisis of faith." Aileen Fyfe and John van Wyhe clarify this state of affairs: "Although much has been made of a mid-Victorian crisis of faith, perhaps triggered by the sciences, this seems to have been a feature of a certain class of intellectuals, and not an accurate description of the majority of society (especially middle-class society), which retained a religious faith long after most expert men of science."[50] It is furthermore impossible to accurately assess the assumed "loss of faith" on the part of the Victorian populace—all social scientists may do is to try to gauge demonstrable actions. While researchers may attempt to track church membership and attendance, "the process of ceasing to believe can never be fully chronicled."[51]

In addition to the problems of quantifying belief, another important issue arises when considering the so-called Victorian faith crisis. John Hedley Brooke suggests that the idea that science and religion, which are terms that defy simple definition, are not implacable enemies but have been so cast in simple analyses of secularization. Such an oppositional treatment ignores the problematic of defining the terms "science" and "religion" and disregards the ways in which both have overlapped. Indeed, *the* relationship between religion and science does not exist; what may be examined is "what different individuals have made of it [the relationship] in a plethora of contexts."[52] Since many tomes have been dedicated to analyses of the ever-shifting connections between science and religion, this chapter can only suggest the difficulties of a uncomplicated assessment of late Victorian secularization.[53]

Whatever its role in the changing faith climate, successful demonstrations of science's power astonished people with its ability to correctly foresee such events. One notable occasion was the appearance of a comet in 1758, which took place just as Edward Halley predicted.[54] Simultaneously, the new scholarly methodology of historical criticism began to destabilize the authority of the

Christian scriptures, a problem especially for Protestants with their stance of *sola scriptura*. Perhaps in an attempt to counterbalance these cultural and intellectual shifts, some Victorians embarked on a search for significance and meaning beyond what their mainline churches could offer. One of the ways in which this quest took shape was interest in the supernatural.[55]

Spiritualist activities, such as séances and church services designed to contact the dead, experienced an enormous wave of popularity in England between 1850 and 1870; a notable interest in mesmerism in the 1830s and 1840s preceded this trend.[56] Historians point to Swedenborg's writings, first published in England in 1845, and mesmerism as matrices of the spiritualist movement in Britain.[57] While the reasons for this upsurge in popularity are varied and complex, clearly by the 1890s spiritualism generated a great allure for many of the educated class.[58]

Highly regarded Victorian professionals, including professors and scientists, among them Fellows of the Royal Society, lent their backing to psychical research, which they envisioned as an exciting new area of science.[59] "In the hands of impartial truth-seekers, the scientific method would open a path into the occult and reduce its seemingly erratic and haphazard character.... Accordingly, many people practiced and investigated the occult in a 'scientific' manner. Mesmerists conducted experiments...and [s]piritualists kept careful record of what unfolded in their séances."[60] Spiritualists and occultists objected not to the scientific method per se, but rather to scientism, which puts forth a mechanistic worldview and holds that only through science may one adjudicate truth.[61] Leading

Victorian spiritualists sought to establish the incorporeal realm as the animator of matter, using similar empirical methods to those employed by the materialistic scientists.[62] There were those in the spiritualist camp, though, who did not believe that the spirit could be measured in the same way as physical objects and remonstrated against the use of the scientific method to quantify spirit.

While Victorian spiritualism appealed to a wide swathe of the population, aficionados of occultism at the *fin de siècle* gathered together in select, elite, and sometimes secret societies.[63] These more intimate groups did not focus on communicating with the dead. Rather, they were drawn together by the promise of initiation, secret teachings, magical ceremonies, and ultimately self-illumination and adepthood. The Theosophical Society (TS), founded in New York in 1875, became the most popular of these groups. It is hard to conceive, though, of Theosophy experiencing the success it did without spiritualism to pave the way in many respects. One wonders if the founders of the Theosophical Society, the Russian Helena Petrovna Blavatsky and the American Colonel Henry Steel Olcott (1832-1907), would have ever crossed paths without their common interest in spiritualism.[64]

Scholars have traditionally argued that the Victorian occult revival was based on a retreat into an irrational and imaginary realm, created as a bulwark for those yearning for firmer existential ground in the face of immense cultural shifts. More recent theories of occultism, tendered by scholars such as Frances Yates and Antoine Faivre, debunk this viewpoint, positing magic as a sound ontology in its own right. Alison Butler also contends that the magical worldview undergirding occultism is coherent and rational, and not merely an escapist strategy in the face of encroaching scientism. In Butler's assessment, the Frazerian conception of magic as inferior, held without question by academics in general until recently, is erroneous. To briefly summarize, Sir James Frazer (1854-1941) argued that civilization underwent a triadic progression of magic, religion, and science. Early humans employed sympathetic magic as a means of ordering their world and control the capricious forces of nature. Eventually, human society progressed to institutionalized religion in an attempt to achieve the same goals. Science, which stood at the zenith of this three-fold sequence, would eventually reign supreme, as the earlier two archaic categories of magic and religion fell away. [65]

As scholarship in the anthropology of religion and related fields has improved over the years, Frazer's theories have lost support in the academy; clearly, modernity is not synonymous with positivism and secularism, and, vice versa, the occult sciences are not inherently at odds with rationality.[66] Faivre sees occultism primarily as the product of the interaction of traditional occult philosophy and scientism in the nineteenth century. As a heterogeneous "counter-current" that developed in reaction to materialistic positivism, occultism sought to amalgamate the *philosophia occulta* with scientific advances.[67] Clearly, occult practitioners of this period saw their magical and spiritual work as a kind of science using definable but oft-hidden cosmic laws, as revealed in the "signatures of nature," the system of correspondences that weaves the world into an organic wholeness.[68] Thus occultism, in its followers' estimation, operated not from a locus of faith but from a scientific foundation, with the Theosophists, for example, understanding science and religion as facets of a unitary philosophy. Critics, on the other hand, saw this as an inappropriate and baseless attempt at the cooption of modern science by the spiritualists.

Historians have noted the ways in which the strain of mass societal changes also fed the Victorian tendency to hyperbolize the mysteries of Oriental cultures, among them India and Tibet. A certain Victorian attraction for obscure sects, Gothic and medieval motifs, and ancient civilizations also lent themselves to Theosophy's popularity. Moreover, "[t]he Theosophical Society thus emerged at a time when discussion of the world's major religions and exposure to Eastern sacred texts were part of educated Victorian cultural life."[69] By and large, the TS consisted of the privileged and well-informed that conversed with ease about novel and burgeoning fields like anthropology, comparative religion, psychology, and sociology.

In addition to occult societies, other significant factions of the time included social justice movements promulgating vegetarianism, anti-vivisection, and feminism. Occult groups drew many of these social activists, appearing more amenable to such concerns than did mainline clergy (although many parishioners of more traditional churches supported women's suffrage).[70] The TS and other like-minded groups even offered more receptivity to feminism and emancipation than did the socialist organizations of the time.[71] As early as June 1911, Theosophy displayed its explicit connections with feminism when Besant and other TS members marched in the Women's Coronation Procession for suffrage, held in London, dressed in "full Masonic regalia" and "under the banner of Universal Co-Masonry." Not surprisingly, recent studies show that a high proportion of prominent Edwardian feminists joined the TS.[72] In late nineteenth-century Britain, the vast majority of women were not admitted to most professional occupations or to the leading universities. Theosophy offered a venue in which women held high offices and wielded power in ways almost unheard of in other British institutions, thus holding great appeal for "the New Woman" of the 1890s.[73]

In addition to the enthrallment with arcana, the 1880s and 1890s saw a renewed curiosity in both Roman Catholic and Protestant circles about the mystical Christianity of earlier times, specifically in the medieval period and the Renaissance. Thus, the Liberal Catholic Church became one of several groups offering alternatives to traditional Christian theology and practice. The publication of a number of influential works marked this period, including Anna Kingsford and Edward Maitland's *The Perfect Way* (1882), William Inge's *Christian Mysticism* in 1899, and Besant's *Esoteric Christianity* (1901). In 1911, Evelyn Underhill, formerly affiliated with Arthur Edward Waite's magical order,[74] published her ever-popular book, *Mysticism*. Underhill had abandoned her work as a ceremonial magician, turning instead to a mystical approach of her native faith that was very much along the lines of Kingsford's work.[75]

Currents of Christian mysticism did exist in the TS, although Blavatsky made her scorn for traditional forms of Judaism and Christianity explicit, writing that..."*real* Theosophy—i.e., the Theosophy that comes to us *from the East*—is assuredly Pantheism and by no means Theism."[76] Tensions between Christian Theosophists and the Eastern-looking TS eventually led to the formation of several offshoot occult groups that focused primarily on Western traditions, most notably the Hermetic Society and the Anthroposophical Society.

Anna Kingsford (1846-1888), formerly an officer in the TS, founded the Hermetic Society in 1884. A convert to Roman Catholicism in her twenties, Kingsford enrolled in the Paris Medical School, since women were not allowed to take medical degrees in Britain at the time, and graduated in 1880. A forthright advocate of Pythagoreanism, anti-vivisection and reincarnation, she penned *The Perfect Way* in 1882, which claimed to be a "new, revealed gospel," based on her many mystical visions. Kingsford held that the Christian revelation was not higher than those of other religions and Jesus was not a unique avatar or divine incarnation, a stance that differentiated her from earlier Christian theosophists such as Jacob Boehme and Louis-Claude de Saint-Martin. Her seminal philosophy drew on "Christianity, Renaissance magic, Eastern mysticism, and late Victorian feminism."[77]

Kingsford joined the TS and in 1883 became president of the British Theosophical Society.[78] During the first year of her office, however, her advocacy of a new Christian esotericism lead to a simmering rivalry with A.P. Sinnett, another Theosophical leader who wanted the TS to focus solely on Eastern philosophies. The dissension between the two visions led to Kingsford's quitting of the TS. Both spiritual partner Edward Maitland (1824-1897) and the scholar A.E. Waite followed her out of the TS, and assisted her in founding the Hermetic Society in 1884. Kingsford's seminal work influenced Theosophical writers Alice Bailey and C. W. Leadbeater, who later borrowed many of her ideas without crediting her.[79]

Annie Besant (1847-1933) joined the TS in 1889, impressed by *The Secret Doctrine* and inspired by her first encounter with Blavatsky that same year. Besant's life before Theosophy paralleled Kingsford's in many ways: both were married to Anglican priests, publicly campaigned for social justice causes and held degrees in science at a time when women rarely pursued such studies—Besant an honors BSc in botany and Kingsford a medical degree. Most importantly in light of this book's subject, Kingsford and Besant promoted Christian mysticism within the TS.

Shortly after the election of Annie Besant to the TS's presidency in 1907, several British lodges incorporated "devotional services" in addition to lectures into their weekly programs, among them the West London Lodge. In 1909 the North London Lodge replaced the regular weekday talks with Sunday night services that included "music, invocations, ethical hymns and addresses." Additionally, a Sunday devotional gathering became a regular occurrence at TS headquarters in Tavistock Square.[80] Later in this chapter, it will be shown Besant was an early champion of the Liberal Catholic Church and the TS's leanings toward more devotional practices during her early presidency presaged the founding and growth of the LCC.

Another Christian theosophical group sprang up after Besant's appointment to the TS. Rudolf Steiner (1861-1925), the general secretary of the German TS branch, broke with the Besant in 1912 over her and Leadbeater's promulgation of Jiddu Krishnamurti as the Coming World-Teacher. In 1912, many German Theosophists, also disgruntled with the World-Teacher scenario, decamped from the TS and organized a new occult assembly. Steiner's newly-formed group, the Anthroposophical Society, commenced with meetings in 1913. In 1922 Steiner oversaw the founding of a sacramental church, the Christian Community, which is still active internationally.[81]

Part Three: The Origins
of the Liberal Catholic Church

The dawning of the Liberal Catholic Church (LCC) officially began in 1916, as detailed in Part One of this chapter, when the Old Catholic Church was restructured in the wake of Mathew's pastoral letter. The ecclesia first adopted the name of the "Old Catholic Church in England;" later it assumed the moniker of the "Liberal Christian Church." In 1918, the leaders decided upon the title of the "Liberal Catholic Church," and that has remained its name ever since.

James Wedgwood (1883-1951) penned a brief but excellent history of the early years of the LCC, first published in *UBIQUE Magazine* in 1937.[82] He also wrote a short autobiography that appeared in the Adyar Bulletin and was reprinted in *Theosophy in New Zealand* (1916). In the latter, Wedgwood recalls being attracted to ritual as a young boy. His grandfather, Hensleigh Wedgwood, was at the forefront of the Spiritualist Alliance and a member of the Society for Psychical Research. Wedgwood had heard about spiritualism and Theosophy when he was quite young: his mother was an accomplished clairvoyant and knew Blavatsky. In his teens, after reading, as phrased it, "a silly little Protestant book," *The Secret History of the Oxford Movement*,[83] Wedgwood became on fire with the idea of joining "the supposedly secret societies" the author so disparaged. He was a member of the Confraternity of the Blessed Sacrament, an Anglo-Catholic organization begun in 1857, as well as other Anglo-Catholic groups.[84]

After university, he embarked on the road to Anglican priesthood and boarded in York with Rev. Patrick Shaw, the vicar of All Saints, North Street. While living on the church premises, Wedgwood had occasion to hear Mrs. Besant lecture in York. She so electrified him that he soon after joined the Theosophical Society, a move that caused him to be "summarily banished from the church." Rev. Shaw would no longer allow Wedgwood to live in the rectory due to his keen interest in the TS. The Painsthorpe Anglican Benedictine monastery, only a few miles from York, became Wedgwood's refuge. The monastery's abbot, Aelred Carlyle, often discussed philosophy with the young man and tried to convince Wedgwood that the Church's system of mysticism was far sounder than that of Theosophy.[85] No longer caring about a church career, though, Wedgwood moved to London and threw himself into working full-time for the TS, living off the trust fund bequeathed to him by his wealthy family. Between 1911 and 1913, he held the position of General Secretary of the TS in England and Wales and in 1913 took on the additional responsibility of Grand Secretary of the British Jurisdiction of the Universal Co-Masonic order.[86]

Perusing a London paper one day, Wedgwood noticed a letter from Rev. Arnold Harris Mathew about ornithology, one of Mathew's great passions. Wedgwood had heard of Mathew's work and wrote to him to inquire about the Old Catholic Church. He unburdened his full autobiography to Mathew and sent him a copy of Annie Besant's book, *Theosophy* (1912).

Wedgwood reminisced:

> "In 1913 a letter appeared in one of the
> London daily newspapers dealing with the
> habits of birds. The letter caught my eye
> especially because it was signed by
> Archbishop A. H. Mathew, of whose exis-
> tence as an Old Catholic bishop in England I
> knew vaguely. Something impelled me to
> write to him to ask for particulars of the
> Church of which he was head. He sent a very
> friendly answer. The idea of taking Orders
> re-entered my head. I told him something of
> the story of my life, of my interest in church
> work and of the studies I had made. During
> the interchange of letters that followed I was
> honest with him about my relation with the
> Theosophical Society, and as some indication
> of one's belief sent him a copy of Mrs.
> Besant's little book, *Theosophy*, published in
> the Jack series of The People's Books. He
> asked me to go and see him, and at once
> accepted me."[87]

Mathew baptized and confirmed Wedgwood *sub conditione*. The young man then took minor orders (subdeacon
and deacon) and was ordained to the priesthood in July
1913. Anson believes that Wedgwood, even after his
move to the TS, never lost his connection to Anglo-
Catholicism and still longed to be a priest.[88]

At the invitation of Mrs. Besant, Wedgwood traveled to
Adyar, the headquarters of the TS, in 1914. From India,
he sailed to Australia in 1915, called there primarily

because of his leadership role in Universal Co-Masonry. While in Australia, he met Charles Webster Leadbeater (1854-1934), a prominent Theosophist and former Anglican priest, and initiated him into Co-Masonry. The two occultists also discussed at length Wedgwood's Old Catholic ordination and the church's activities under Archbishop Mathew.

While traveling back to England from Australia in the summer later that year, Wedgwood heard about two calamities racking his home church. Mathew had dismissed his co-adjucator, Bishop Willoughby, due to the publication of a piece in a London weekly periodical condemning Willoughby's character (generally accepted to be a veiled charge of homosexuality). The second crisis was the aforementioned contentious pastoral epistle of 6 August 1915 no longer allowing church members to be connected to Theosophy.[89]

The upshot of this communiqué, as earlier discussed, was that the entire band of Mathew's clergy with the exception of Rupert Gauntlett (who was seriously considering submission to Rome) stood united with the TS members in breaking with Mathew. Although Wedgwood and the other clergy formerly affiliated with Mathew were not enthusiastic to found another church, they felt some obligation to the dedicated and sincere laity who left Mathew's congregation along with them. On February 13, 1916, the London Co-Masonic Temple was the scene of Wedgwood's consecration to the bishopric, with Willoughby administering the sacrament and presiding over the large congregation who gathered for the event. Wedgwood became the presiding bishop of the new church, initially named "the Old Catholic Church of

England."[90] Later that year, Wedgwood once again landed on the shores of Australia; in July, he consecrated Leadbeater as the second bishop in the newly constituted church.

Leadbeater, a former Anglican clergyman with an interest in spiritualism, had joined the TS in 1883. After the deaths of Blavatsky and Olcott, Besant ascended to the presidency of the TS in 1907; by the 1890s Leadbeater became Besant's occult magister and most trusted advisor. Indeed, for decades, the majority of the TS held Leadbeater up as the pre-eminent occultist after the death of Blavatsky. Few characters in twentieth-century religious history bring up the extreme range of reactions inspired by Leadbeater. There are those who glorify him as "a self-illumined man"[91] and great occultist and those who disparage him as a pedophile as well as a power-hungry charlatan. What is undeniable is the influence of Leadbeater's prodigious literary works, which include over 65 books and innumerable articles. Many of his most important works, including *The Hidden Side of Things* and *The Inner Life* are still in print and his *oeuvre* has had an inestimable influence on modern theosophy and New Age spirituality.

Leadbeater's younger years are to some extent mysterious. He related many colorful tales of his childhood and the veracity of these stories is uncertain. His pre-eminent biographer says that Leadbeater "was not adverse to rewriting the past to suit his own requirements, be it the evolutionary past of man on this planet, the past lives of his friends and enemies, or the humbler history of his own family."[92] It is known for sure that he was ordained to the Anglican deaconate in Britain in 1878 and served as an assistant curate in a parish in Bramshott, Hampshire. After being ordained a priest in 1879, he joined the Confraternity of the Blessed Sacrament in 1882, which was somewhat surprising since the parish at which he served as curate was Low Church.

In 1884, shortly after joining the TS, Leadbeater received a psychic communiqué from one of the Masters, Koot Hoomi, to travel to India, an instruction he followed within three days. After arriving at TS's headquarters in Adyar, India, his duties primarily entailed preparing the monthly journal *The Theosophist* for publication and handling correspondence for the Society. Also in 1884, Leadbeater resigned from the Confraternity of the Blessed Sacrament and took Buddhist vows of refuge. A tall, imposing man with a full beard, impressive mane of hair, and twinkling eyes, he became progressively more well-known and respected in the TS, taking on the position of editing *The Buddhist*, an English language periodical. During this period, Tillett reports that Leadbeater became increasing hostile to Christianity, even going so far as to burn an Anglican catechism at a TS meeting in 1886.[93]

By 1894, his great lifelong friendship with Besant began to blossom. Besant was one of the very few women whose presence he tolerated; his virulent misogyny was infamous. She repaid his friendship with unflagging allegiance, standing by his side throughout the scandals that dogged his career. In spite of Besant's firm faith in her mentor and advisor, certain factions of the Society found Leadbeater of highly dubious moral integrity. Accusations of immoral and inappropriate conduct with young boys were repeatedly lodged against him throughout his life. In addition, many Theosophists questioned his authenticity as a clairvoyant and Initiate. In February 1909, when Besant allowed Leadbeater to rejoin the TS after he had resigned two years earlier amid charges of pedophilia, her decision portended a mass exodus of TS members. G.R.S. Mead, a highly regarded scholar and formerly Blavatsky's amanuensis, left the Society in protest following this incident, along with several hundred other British Theosophists.

Over the decades, the various spirited campaigns attempting to dislodge Leadbeater as Besant's top advisor failed one after another. One notable incident was the publicly published letter from TS member T.H. Martyn[94] on 21 May 1921, charging both Wedgwood and Leadbeater with immoral sexual practices (homosexuality and pedophilia, respectively) and questioning their status as initiates. Besant fired back a general letter to the TS in support of both the bishops. As always, Besant stood by Leadbeater no matter what the charges against him. Always a staunch supporter of the Liberal Catholic Church, she envisioned it as one of the "Three Activities" undertaken to prepare for the Coming World-Teacher (along with the Theosophical Education Trust and Co-Masonry).[95] Even though women could not aspire to clerical orders in the LCC, Besant was an unwavering benefactor of the fledgling church from its very inception, often writing articles for its monthly journal and offering benedictions from the high altar during services. Her essay on transubstantiation is printed in the book, *The Occultism of the Mass* (1918).[96]

To be sure, ceremonialism and Theosophy were tightly linked during the quarter-century that Besant and Leadbeater headed the TS. In the early 1900s, a "ceremo-

nial revival" took root in England, with Theosophists joining magical and ritual groups in significant numbers.
Wedgwood and Besant were long-time devotees of ceremonial theurgical work, which uses liturgy, ritual, vestments, prayers, and consecrated implements to facilitate
and direct spiritual energies in specific ways.
Intermediaries, like angels and planetary rulers, are often
invoked to assist in this process. Besant was affiliated with
Le Droit Humain, the French Masonic movement that
accepted both women and men into its lodges; she served
on the *Le Droit Humain* Supreme Council for 30 years, and
was of the earliest members of British Universal Co-
Masonry (which also allows both sexes to join) beginning
in 1902. With the enthusiastic support of Besant, James
Wedgwood, a Co-Mason as well as member of other
Masonic, Martinist and occult groups, and Marie Russak,
also a Co-Mason, established a ceremonial order called
the Temple of the Rosy Cross in 1912.[97]

As noted previously, Wedgwood inducted Leadbeater
into Co-Masonry in June 1915, after convincing
Leadbeater that an intrinsic part of the coming age would
be ceremonial work. Leadbeater swiftly ascended to the
highest Masonic degree and became an officer in the
Australian Co-Masonry order. Eventually Leadbeater
would assume a central role within numerous ancillary
occult organizations of the TS, including the OSE, the
Golden Chain, the Lotus Circle, and the Order of the
Round Table.[98]

Wedgwood also won over Leadbeater to the mission of
Old Catholicism. During another visit to Australia in
1916, Wedgwood administered baptism, confirmation,
and ordination to minor orders and the priesthood *sub*

conditione to Leadbeater at the residence of a prominent TS member, Johnkheer Julian Mazel on 15 July.[99] Six days later, Wedgwood consecrated Leadbeater as a bishop of the "Old Roman Catholic Church of England."

The formation of this Christian church led and sanctioned by Theosophical luminaries moved the TS even farther away from the organization created by Blavatsky and Olcott. The formation of the LCC elicited strong criticism from various sectors of the TS. Charles J. Ryan writes that, "Another cause of anxiety and loss of membership [of the TS, in addition to Leadbeater's moral indiscretions] arose from the opposition to Mrs. Besant's encouragement of the Liberal Catholic Church and the Co-Masonic Order, in both of which Mr. Leadbeater became strongly interested as a high official. Many theosophical workers considered such undertakings quite out of place in close association with the Theosophical Society.... They thought the identification of many well-known members with those extraneous activities compromised the non-sectarian character of the Society."[100] In spite of such opposition, Besant, Leadbeater, and Wedgwood continued to uphold the LCC as a major component of the Theosophical mission.

Part Four: The Development of the Liberal Catholic Church

After Leadbeater's consecration in 1916, the LCC's two bishops took up their first task, the writing of the new Church's liturgy. Mindful of maintaining the church's connection to Christianity even while incorporating an occult theology, Wedgwood declared: "Ours was a Christian church and we intended to keep it such."[101] Aiming to retain much of the traditional Roman Catholic liturgy, they developed the rites based on *The Old Catholic Missal and Ritual*, published by Bishop Arnold Harris Mathew in 1909 with an imprimatur from Geraldus Gul, the Archbishop of Utrecht.[102] Leadbeater's clairvoyant communiqués with a Master in the Theosophical hierarchy known as the Count, or Prince Rakoczy, were an integral part of the creative process. The Count, according to Leadbeater, had incarnated as St. Alban, Francis Bacon, Christian Rosenkreutz, and other august personages throughout history. Through their frequent psychic conversations, the Count guided the formation of the liturgy and answered Leadbeater's various ecclesial queries via their psychic conversations.[103]

In this new version of the liturgy, any allusions to God's wrath, eternal damnation or petitions for clemency fell by the wayside; the Theosophical bishops emphasized co-operation with God rather than entreaties to Him. The first version came out in 1918 and included the liturgies for the Mass and other services, including Vespers and Communion of the Sick. By 1919, the LCC published the full edition of the liturgy.[104]

Leadbeater laid out the church's mission and rationale in 1917, explaining that the Old Catholic Church appealed to those who have "intellectual difficulties" with traditional Christianity's dogma but still wish to receive the sacraments. In fact, as James Santucci avers, "The Church under Wedgwood became in effect the Theosophical section of the Old Catholic Church."[105] While the church allowed the "widest measure of liberty in the interpretation of the Scriptures, the creeds and the liturgy," Liberal Catholic faith is grounded in the

Scriptures and traditional Christian creeds. Following the traditions of the Roman Catholic Church, the LCC recognizes both Tradition and Holy Scripture as divine revelation, administers the seven sacraments and maintains the apostolic succession. The preservation of the apostolic succession is of particular importance, as is the proper administration of the sacraments; both of these must be in place for the sacraments to be efficacious.[106]

The LCC envisioned itself as a full member of the body of Christ as manifested in the One, Holy, Catholic, and Apostolic Church. Leadbeater explains, "The idea of belonging to a separate Church or to an independent sect was always most repugnant to the Old Roman Catholics of Holland, from whom our episcopal succession is derived."[107] The LCC sought to exist harmoniously with other churches and offered an open table policy in regard to communion: All those of good will, irrespective of their religious affiliation, might partake of the Eucharist. As far as polity, the LCC maintained the episcopal model, with candidates for the bishopric being elected by the General Episcopal Synod.[108]

Even though Wedgwood and Leadbeater founded the LCC upon the principles of complete doctrinal freedom for its members, a specific theological stance underpinned the Church, primarily informed by Theosophical teachings and Leadbeater's psychic researches and realizations. Voluminous theological writings, for the most part penned by Leadbeater, Wedgwood, LCC priest Geoffrey Hodson (1886-1983), and Bishop Irving Pigott, articulate the Church's position in great detail. While the teachings of the LCC are too intricate to cover here in depth, the following summarizes some of the primary motifs.

One of the Church's central teachings holds that a divine essence resides in every being, and after proceeding through the cycles of reincarnation, each being will realize that divinity. This concept of inevitable salvation is similar to Origen's Platonist doctrine of the *apokatastasis* (*restitutio in pristinum statum,* restoration to the pristine state) in which universal salvation is achieved by all of creation.[109]

In order to reawaken this spark of divinity, Liberal Catholicism advises active participation in the sacramental life of the Church, primarily the Eucharist. Participation in the sacraments purifies the seven interpenetrating subtle and gross "sheaths" or bodies[110] that comprise the human body and the pace of spiritual evolution is hastened. Instrumental in this process is the cooperation of intermediary beings such as angels, who are drawn by the subtle thought forms generated during the performance of the sacraments. Leadbeater delineates this complex metaphysical liturgiology in *The Science of the Sacraments*, an imposing 560-page tome first published in 1920.[111]

According to Leadbeater, the chief LCC theologian, the Church's principal purpose is to "co-operate with the Angel agents of God in the manipulation of mighty unseen, but very beneficent, forces."[112] The primary vehicle for this cooperative working is the Mass. The Eucharist, as the focus of the Mass, has a substantive energetic effect on the subtle and material planes; each time the Eucharist is celebrated, peace and strength go forth into the world and the environs of the church are purified. Church worship, in Liberal Catholicism's estimation, should not emphasize dogmatic preaching or the personal salvation and consolation of the congregants. Worshippers should concentrate on assisting one's fellow humans in their spiritual evolution, the latter being another basic tenet of Theosophy.

This evolutionary process is enhanced during the Mass by the creation of the Eucharistic edifice, a form of coalesced mental energy that receives, grounds, and transfers Holy Energy. This edifice, which also may be thought of as a vehicle or container, is constructed on the mental, astral, etheric, and higher planes during the Mass. This feat is accomplished through the effects of the liturgy, aided by the conscious participation of the congregants as well as angelic beings. During a potent Mass, especially a high service with music and incense, Leadbeater and other clairvoyants report perceiving a huge multi-colored thought-form towering over the physical church building.[113]

Ultimately, the Liberal Catholic Mass is conceived as a theurgical act and as such is remarkably similar to magical operations in other ceremonial settings. Joscelyn Godwin remarks of Leadbeater: "At heart he was a magician, and the Mass was his preferred rite of ceremonial magic."[114] Liberal Catholicism understands each of the sacraments as a theurgical undertaking, which Leadbeater elucidated in detail in *The Science of the Sacraments*. For example, the primary effect of baptism is that the incipient good qualities in the unformed astral and mental bodies of the child may be stimulated and the tendencies for evil may be deadened. This "act of white magic" opens certain chakras (subtle energy centres). It consecrates the subtle and gross bodies of the child, so that the soul may be truly expressed and it may be dedicated to the service of the Holy.[115]

For Liberal Catholics, the Christian path, properly understood and practiced, is one efficacious method to achieve this enlightened state, although by no means the only one. The LCC strongly disagrees with traditional Christological formulations positing Jesus as the only Son of God and the sole redeemer of a fallen humanity. Rather, proceeding from a universalistic view of religion inspired by Theosophy, the Liberal Catholics believe that "Master Jesus" is one of several empowered incarnations or avatars that have appeared on this planet to assist humans in their evolution. Periodically, these avatars appear as envoys of the Christ energy, designated to teach and exemplify the enlightened life to the human race. Jesus became such a carrier for the Christ energy at the age of 29; therefore, Jesus the man is distinguished from the Christ Energy (or the Christos) that he embodied during the last few years of his life, another Theosophical tenet.[116]

Mainline Christians familiar with the LCC's metaphysical leanings tend to scoff at its philosophy. One writer railed, "No more bizarre religious concoction can be imagined than the wedding of sacramentalism and Theosophy in Liberal Catholicism.... A Roman Catholic instinctively views the sect as a fantastic religious nightmare."[117] And not only were traditional Christians dismayed—as noted before, the LCC created rancor in the TS, even though officially the two groups were administratively separate. Godwin wittily remarks, "Blavatsky, too, must have turned in Devaloka to see the religion she detested taking over her Society."[118] In the 1920s, the Society and the LCC would erupt over this and other related issues with catastrophic consequences for both organizations.

Part Five: The Liberal Catholic Church and Krishnamurti

In 1888, thirteen years after the founding of the Theosophical Society, Madame Blavatsky suggested the appearance of what was later to be known as a World-Teacher in the final quarter of the next century. However, it was second-generation Theosophists, most notably Annie Besant and Charles Webster Leadbeater, that viewed the Society as the organization destined to help prepare for the arrival of the World-Teacher, the Vehicle of whom was discovered to be Jiddu Krishnamurti in 1909.

Blavatsky expected the avatar's advent to occur sometime between 1975 and 2000. As early as 1899, though, Annie Besant, a new TS member at the time, began to talk up the World-Teacher project, believing that the next incarnation of the Christ Energy on earth would be foreshadowed by a new sub-race of humans with amplified psychic powers.[119] Besant defined the role of the Coming Teacher thus: "The World-Teacher is the founder of a religion, preaching again the ancient basic Truths which all great religions have in common, but giving them a form adapted to the time...."[120]

In December 1908, Besant, who had assumed the TS presidency after Olcott's death in 1907, believed that the new sub-race had begun to take birth and thus announced the imminent coming of the World-Teacher. She would not have to wait very long for the "Vehicle" of Lord Maitreya[121] to appear. In fact, he was discovered a few months later on the South Indian seashore.[122]

Jiddu Krishnamurti (1895-1986) was recognized to be the "Coming World-Teacher" in a most unusual manner.

In April 1909 on the beach at Adyar, India, Leadbeater observed the adolescent Krishnamurti (also known as Krishna) playing in the waves of the Bay of Bengal with his younger brother, Nityananda. Leadbeater, who was a TS leader and generally recognized as the most able clairvoyant channel between the Masters and the Society, resided in the TS's Adyar headquarters. When Leadbeater introduced Krishna to Besant in September 1909, she concurred with his high estimation of Krishna's potential.[123] With the permission of their father, eventually Besant became the ward of the two brothers, who were then brought to England for education with a view to grooming Krishna for his role as World-Teacher.

Meanwhile, Besant's policies as TS president were upsetting a fair number of Theosophists; especially rankling to many was her utter reliance on and faith in Leadbeater's advice, visions, and communiqués from the Masters. Leadbeater, a highly prolific writer and self-proclaimed medium, was the most influential figure in the Adyar TS after Besant. Some in the inner circles of the Society also objected to Besant and Leadbeater's championing of Krishna as avatar, including Rudolf Steiner, secretary of the German TS, and Katherine Tingley, the outspoken leader of the Point Loma Theosophists. The rancor against Krishna increased after the founding of the Order of the Star of the East (OSE) in 1911. Primarily consisting of Theosophists and headed by Krishna, this new association drew together those dedicated to preparing for the World-Teacher's arrival. The standoff between Besant and Steiner regarding the World-Teacher came to a head in 1912, with Steiner and most of the German Theosophists departing the TS to eventually form a new esoteric organization, the

Anthroposophical Society, as well assisting some of his followers in founding another esoteric sacramental church, the *Christengemeinschaft* (Christian Community). Another thorn in the side of numerous Theosophists was Besant and Leadbeater's close involvement with the Liberal Catholic Church, as discussed earlier. Another Theosophist who departed the Society was Dion Fortune (Violet Mary Firth), who established an occult order in 1928 as well as a church under the name, "The Guild of Master Jesus."[124]

As a TS leader and head of the OSE, Krishna was forced to endure a wide array of ritual functions. By 1921, at the age of 26, Krishna had begun to come into his own as a spiritual leader and felt free to publicly express his opinions, which sometimes ran afoul of the TS party line. This was particularly obvious in Krishna's distaste for rituals and ceremonies. The next year, in 1922, Lady Emily received a letter from Krishna describing a 2½-hour long Liberal Catholic service he had attended led by Leadbeater: "He did it all very well but you know I am not a ceremonialist and I do not appreciate all the paraphanalia [sic] with all those prayers and bobbing up and down, the robes etc."[125]

In November 1925, while Krishna was traveling in Europe with Annie Besant and other inner circle TS members (including George Arundale and James Wedgwood), he received the message that his brother Nitya had died of a longstanding illness. Shortly after his brother's passing, Krishna openly began to expound teachings radically at odds with his occult indoctrination under the guidance of Leadbeater and Besant. Along with rituals and ceremonial work, he rejected the traditional occult system of initiation and the TS's emphasis on the relationship between guru and *chela* (disciple), all of which he saw as superfluous to spiritual awakening and even as obstacles to realization.[126] These publicly declaimed ideas signaled Krishna's clear intention to reform the TS and eventually led to his disassociation with Theosophy.

Even today, speculation continues to swirl around Krishnamurti's volte-face after his sibling's death. Whatever the reason, Krishna continued to "deconstruct" Theosophy, with Besant's tacit sanction continually undercutting Leadbeater's authority. In the midst of the resultant upheaval caused by Krishna's novel philosophy, Besant announced that finally Lord Maitreya had spoken through Krishna: "In 1925, came the first public manifestation that he [Krishna] was the chosen vehicle of the World-Teacher, on the 28th day of December, the Star Anniversary...." This pronouncement of the "overshadowing," as the event came to be known, only caused the fierce struggles for power within upper levels of the TS to intensify—the primary characters in this ongoing mêlée were Leadbeater on one side and Wedgwood and George Arundale on the other. So tired was Besant of the TS's turmoil and seamy politics she even considered resigning her presidency in 1925, in order to follow Krishna as an ordinary disciple.[127]

As one might imagine, Krishna's revolutionary philosophy greatly upset the TS's equilibrium. In 1927, with Besant's approval, he terminated all ritual-based practices of the OSE, including the awarding of grades, badges, and sashes. When queried about his attitude toward ceremonial groups, Krishna replied: "I have been asked why I do not concern myself with certain movements. Am I antagonistic to them? I am not antagonistic to anyone or any movement.... It is more important to break the bondages that constrain life, than to create new forms, new phantasies, new phantoms to be worshipped."

Leadbeater tried to salvage the problematic and embarrassing situation in the TS resulting from Krishna's novel teachings, so at odds with his own. Leadbeater attempted to manage the situation in two principal ways: 1) By asserting that although the World-Teacher manifested through Krishna, sometimes he did not, i.e., that Krishna was a fallible Vehicle; and 2) by explaining that Krishna's role was to be a strong proponent of the mystical path, a different yet equal path from the occult path.

Leadbeater's endorsement of the "twin paths" of occultism and mysticism had antecedents in Theosophical circles. For example, Annie Besant sketched out the two spiritual methodologies in 1919:

> "The Occultist and the Mystic differ in their methods as well as in their object. The Occultist seeks knowledge of God; the Mystic seeks union with God. The Occultist uses Intellect; the Mystic Emotion . . . These sharp-cut definitions are, of course, true only of abstract types; the concrete individuals shade off into each other, and the perfected Occultist finally includes the Mystic, the perfected Mystic finally includes the Occultist . . . Blessed, holy and necessary are both types, the two Hands of the One LOGOS in His helping of His universe."[128]

In any event, Krishna ignored Leadbeater's twin path theory and carried on with his scathing criticisms of ceremonialism.

Leadbeater's strategy in proposing the mystic and occult methods as complementary failed to calm the confusion in the LCC. During 1927 and 1930, its members, along with those in the TS and the OSE (and often one person would belong to all three organizations), suffered through uncertainty and bewilderment. Krishna's admonitions to give up ceremonialism placed LCC clergy and parishioners in a difficult predicament, perplexed about whose direction to follow: Krishna, whom they had accepted as the World-Teacher; or Leadbeater, their presiding bishop, who had previously given Krishna the highest endorsement. Besant, although dedicated to ritual work and sympathetic to Leadbeater, sided with Krishna in the debate.

Numerous articles written by Leadbeater at the time point up the issues at hand: "Krishnaji himself assures us that he is the World-Teacher and has absolute identification of consciousness with Him ... I know that the World-Teacher often speaks through Krishnaji, but I also know that there are occasions when he does *not*." According to the presiding bishop, this intermittent overshadowing also occurred in the life of Jesus. Leadbeater continues by defining the "twin paths" of the occultist and the mystic. Each of these paths appeals to different people—occultists "develop themselves step by step...and there are those [the mystics] who try to fly straight to the goal without anything intermediate."

In the same article, Leadbeater confides that the energy of the World-Teacher [Lord Maitreya, as distinct from Krishna] "ordered the formation of the LCC, and at the same time...especially energized another scheme of ceremonial called Co-Masonry." And to balance things out,

"Krishnaji is throwing all his energy into giving an

impulse to that Mystic line.... Krishnaji says: 'Ceremonies are unnecessary, throw them away....' Of course they are not necessary, not essential.... But they are sometimes useful for certain purposes. I could do with my will some of the things which a Church or Masonic ceremony does, but it would take me days of hard work to do them. Why should I waste that time and that power when I can produce the same result by a ceremony?" Krishna is so zealously against ceremony because, "He must be entirely one pointed...or he will never strike hard enough to make the necessary impression on a pachydermatous public."

Leadbeater exhorted LCC members to realize while there is only one truth, there are many refractions of this truth: "...[L]et us take the nobler attitude of endeavouring to synthesize, to understand the agreement between them...."[129]

In the midst of this highly debated issue of ceremonialism, Krishna made a speech that rocked the foundations of the Theosophical Society. In a single blow, the thirty-four-year old Brahmin laid waste to the hopes and plans of Besant, Leadbeater, and so many of his followers who looked to him as the incarnation of the Christ energy. On 3 August 1929, from his dais at Ommen, the rural compound of the Order of the Star[130] in Holland, the handsome, charismatic Krishna, groomed for the role of savior since the age of 14, abdicated his position as World-Teacher and dissolved the Order, which at the time had approximately 30,000 members. Although Krishnamurti officially remained in the TS until mid-1930, sorting out administrative details like land trusts, in all practical respects he severed his ties with the organization that day.

Astonishment and outrage reverberated through the TS

and the Order of the Star, and TS members abandoned the Society by the thousands. Many who left, however, continued to be loyal to Krishnamurti and his new vision. His resignation also catapulted the LCC into disorder, although it was officially and administratively separate from both the TS and the Order of the Star. In response to this crisis, the Church convened an Episcopal Synod at Adyar in early 1930. Present were Bishops Leadbeater, Wedgwood, Pigott, Irving Cooper, and Johan Hubert Bonjer, with proxies from several other LCC bishops. In documents released after the conference, the Synod declared: "In regard to the World-Teacher, to our connexion with the TS and other kindred bodies perfect freedom is allowed to our members. And in matters of belief the clergy are now as free as the laity."[131]

Furthermore, the Synod informed parishioners that it had removed any citations about the World-Teacher from the LCC Summary of Doctrine and modified the liturgy so that any references of the "physical return of our Lord" now spoke of the "awakening" of the Christ within the "human heart." The bishops took a neutral position in regard to the World-Teacher question: The Church will not make "an authoritative pronouncement binding the members of the Church to accept Krishnaji as the World-Teacher." The Synod further commented, "We are in the presence here of a Great Mystery—what the early Christians used to call the Mystery of the Incarnation."[132]

Liberal Catholic clergy members, including Pigott and Geoffrey Hodson, tried to come to terms with Krishna's intellectual stance vis-à-vis ceremonies and organizations. Referring to Krishnamurti's New Zealand talks, first published in 1934, Pigott remarks:

"They are very stimulating.... But I cannot follow his argument about ceremonies. He says, for instance, (p. 36): "We might think by attending a church we feel elated, full of vitality and a sense of well being. I am not insulting when I say that by taking to drink you feel the same, or attending a stimulating lecture; but why do you place ceremony as being much more important, more vital, more essential, than appreciation of something which really stimulates you?'... What is the objection [of Krishnamurti]? Personally I do not care for ceremonies, but I love sacraments and put up with church ceremonies for the sake of sacraments. But many others love ceremonies—church, Masonic, civic, military, academic, and whatnot—for their own sake...because they stimulate some part of our amazingly complex being. Well, why not? Krishnamurti never makes this clear to me.... Krishnamurti never seems to me to say anything about sacraments, as distinct from ceremonies, either for or against. I doubt he understands what we mean by the Eucharistic Presence. Either he doesn't understand it or has never heard of it or thinks it unnecessary to mention it."[133]

Hodson, who was an LCC priest in addition to being one of the foremost TS spokespersons, agreed with Pigott's suspicion that Krishnamurti did not understand "the great realities behind Freemasonry" and other ritual work. He finishes his critique of Krishnamurti with this thought: "Lastly, if it is urged that ceremonials and orders are not essential to the fulfilment [sic] of life, I reply: "No intelligent person ever said they were."

As TS intellectuals debated Krishnamurti's philosophy, LCC parishes continued to languish during the early 1930s. In his monthly column in *The Liberal Catholic*, Bishop Pigott lamented: "Baptisms, Confirmations, and Admissions are practically at a standstill." Week by week, according the bishop, the number of congregants lessened, even though the LCC offered them a beautiful church edifice, an accomplished organist, and so forth. Pigott writes that previously, attendance at Sunday morning services was between 150-200, and now a year or two later rarely do more than 100 worshippers show up. Like most churches, the LCC relied on donations, which became fewer and less generous. Finances became so strained that the London parish could not even afford to buy a typewriter for the church office.[134] Two months later, nonetheless, in the June 1930 issue of *The Liberal Catholic*, Pigott rallied, exhorting the faithful to keep working steadily and not to become pessimistic about declining membership. The generous donation of an office typewriter may have renewed his enthusiasm for the mission.[135]

Far-flung correspondents for *The Liberal Catholic* reported the LCC's dwindling numbers in their home churches. For example, Francis of Antioch wrote: "The Church I attended [in the U.S.] was well filled every Sunday morning and evening. Then came "The Star in the East" movement, and we began to dwindle in numbers and enthusiasm till at last...the place where I and my dear ones once worshipped is now almost empty.... There is too much

Krishnaji and not enough Christ Jesus in many so called Liberal Catholics. Liberalism is good, but it may be stretched too far."[136]

In Sydney, a former bastion of the LCC, only a core group of Liberal Catholics remained: "There are not the congregations of the old days when the affairs of the Church were inspired by certain great and dominating personalities, and when the foundations were unshaken by the message of Krishnamurti." Even as far away as the East Indies, Krishnamurti's diatribes against ceremonialism decimated LCC flocks. Rt. Rev. A.G. Vreede, Regionary Bishop for the Netherlands Indies, sent a letter regarding the island of Java: "Up until 1927 our growth was marvelous, then Krishnamurti spoke against churches, etc., in general." Vreede, writing in 1932, reported that the number of congregations had been reduced by about half.[137]

By 1932, Church leaders felt reasonably certain that the exodus of 1927-1930 was over. Bishop Pigott encouraged his remaining congregants, now clustered in small but dedicated groups, to take heart, even in the early stages of recovery for the Church. "We belong essentially to the future though there is so much in our work that is all one with the centuries-old Catholic tradition.... We are in a sense a waiting church, waiting for [the] time that our philosophy...will be understood and appreciated.... Its time is not yet."[138] L.J. Bendit penned a letter to *The Liberal Catholic* concurring with Pigott's vision: "Thus I can see no grounds for pessimism nor for disappointment and a sense of failure. On the contrary, I think we are in a semi-quiescent phase preparatory to one of great activity, in accordance with the great and universally applicable cyclic law of nature."[139]

As the Church slowly regained its footing in the aftermath of the World-Teacher debacle, the global financial troubles of the 1930s added to its difficulties. The small number of active parishioners felt the sharp pinch of the Depression. *The Liberal Catholic* magazine, never fiscally robust, began to lose money; in order to balance the publication's budget, the editor decided to cut down the size of the magazine. Pigott reported "a disappointing response to the Easter Appeal" of 1935, noting that the Church's Central Fund was depleted.[140] The London church was able to make ends meet by renting out its halls, but in general, the numbers of parishioners continued to be stationary, with no new centers being founded and few newcomers attending services.

Ultimately, though, the Liberal Catholic Church survived both Krishnamurti and the Depression. The Theosophical Society has endured the past 75 years as well, although it has never come close to achieving the membership figure of 45,000 it could claim in 1928. Both Besant and Leadbeater died within a few years of Krishnamurti's announcement, in 1933 and 1934 respectively. It seems that most contemporary LCC parishioners and clergy have little knowledge of Krishnamurti's historical connection to their Church. Bishop Maurice Warnon remarks: "Today Liberal Catholics have only slight consideration for this part of the history of their Church [and Krishnamurti], but during the first fifteen years of the life of this Church, it was by far the subject of the greatest concern of many members. Certainly, the initial rapid growth at the beginning of the Liberal Catholic Church was connected in part with the Coming of the World-Teacher. How great were the disappointment and the confusion of these people when they realized that the World-Teacher proved quite different from what they had expected?"[141]

Part Six: The Liberal Catholic Church in the United States

In 1919, James Wedgwood, the presiding bishop of the LCC, along with Charles Leadbeater, consecrated Irving Steiger Cooper (d. 1935) as regionary bishop of the Province of the United States of America. In 1923, Leadbeater took over as presiding bishop of the LCC, and by 1926, three more men were raised as bishops for the American LCC churches. One of these three was Ray Marshall Wardall (d. 1953) and another was John Moynihan Tettemer (1876-1949). Tettemer had formerly served in the Roman Catholic Church, as a priest and monk in the Passionist order. In 1927, became the LCC's Suffragan Bishop for the United States. Married with three children, he lived in Beverly Hills at the end of his life and acted in several movies.[142]

The LCC functioned for almost three decades without a schism, a miraculous record in the Independent Catholic milieu. In the 1940s, however, the denomination was racked by lawsuits, schisms, and defections too complicated to detail here. Anson and Piepkorn both delineate this convoluted state of affairs in their respective tomes.[143] The LCC, even with its attendant schisms, has flourished on an international level, with parishes in Australia, Canada, England, the United States, Western Europe, India, South America, Africa, Cuba, and Scandinavia, and in many other locales. According to Dr. Robert Ellwood, a scholar of religion and an LCC priest: "There are several different Liberal Catholic denominations now, some new and rather fluid, formed basically over the ordination of women issue: the LCC International, one based in the Netherlands, one based in Canada under Bishop [Maurice] Warnon, and the Liberal Catholic Church, under Presiding Bishop Graham Wale in England and with some fifteen churches in this country, including Greeley, CO under Bishop Lloyd Worley, and Ojai, where the Regionary Bishop and I live.... All these LCCs ordain women or appear moving to do so except mine, the last....[144]

Especially important to note is the Liberal Catholic Church's influence, which is felt far beyond its own parishes, since many if not most esoteric sacramental churches trace their origins to this seminal religious body. A notable example is the Gnostic lineage founded by Dr. Ronald Powell (b. 1916-1978),[145] a member of the TS and an LCC priest in Australia. Hugh George de Willmot Newman, who was Metropolitan of Glastonbury and Catholicos of the West, consecrated Powell in 1953. Powell went on to found the Pre-Nicene Gnosto-Catholic Church on 25 October 1953 in London "with the object of restoring the GNOSIS-DIVINE WISDOM to the Christian Church." Around the same time, he changed his name to Richard Jean Crètien, Duc de Palatine.[146]

Some see Palatine as the inaugural force behind the modern Gnostic revival in the English-speaking world; Valentinus, Basilides, Marcion, Paul, and Cerentius inspired his many writings on spiritual topics. His published books include *The Inner Meaning of the Mystery Schools*, *You and Reincarnation*, and *The Great Parable*. He taught that the ancient Christian Gnostics did not view scriptural texts as history but rather as "the presentation of the Spiritual Drama of the Fall of the Divine Man into matter and his eventual return to his original Spiritual Home." Palatine moved to California in the 1960s and founded the Sanctuary of Gnosis in Hollywood, California.[147]

The principal inheritor of Palatine's mantle in the United States is Dr. Stephan A. Hoeller (Tau Stephanus), the presiding bishop of *Ecclesia Gnostica,* which is head-quartered in Los Angeles. Hoeller, originally from Budapest, was raised in Europe during the Second World War, the son of "an Austrian baron and a Hungarian countess." His parents were devoted Roman Catholics and Hoeller studied for the Roman Catholic priesthood in Austria and in Rome. While still a teenager, he started reading early Christian Gnostics like Basilides and Simon Magus. Hoeller received a PhD in philosophy, with minor in philosophy of religion, from an Austrian university. After the war, Hoeller landed in Belgium as a refugee and it was there he first encountered members of a Gnostic Christian group. In 1953, he immigrated to US and set-tled in Los Angeles, where he still resides. Hoeller was ordained in the American Catholic Church in 1958 and founded his own church in Los Angeles in 1959. On 7 April 1967 Richard, Duc de Palatine consecrated Hoeller to the episcopate.[148]

The most well-known and respected Independent Gnostic Catholic prelate in the United States, Hoeller is also a prolific writer and active Theosophist. His books include *The Royal Road: A Manual of Kabalistic Meditations on the Tarot* (1992), *Jung and the Lost Gospels* (1989), *Gnosticism: New Light on the Ancient Tradition of Inner*

Knowing (2002), all published by Quest Books (owned and operated by the Theosophical Society) in Wheaton, Illinois.

Hoeller believes that the Gnostic Mass is different from the Roman Catholic Mass "primarily by way of intentionality." The Mass, Hoeller remarks, is "a mystical, theurgic act which has been given to us by the founder of the Christian religion." While participation in the Mass assists one in attaining gnosis, it is not a reenactment of the crucifixion. Not surprisingly, Hoeller is trained in ceremonial magic and personally knew psychologist Israel Regardie, the author of many tomes on ceremonial magic and amanuensis to the famed occultist Aleister Crowley.[149]

Another influential denomination in the esoteric Independent Catholic world is the Catholic Apostolic Church of Antioch—Malabar Rite, which also holds ancestral links to the LCC as well as to Joseph René Vilatte's lineage. Hermann Adrian Spruit, formerly a Methodist clergyman, was consecrated in 1957 by LCC bishop Charles Hampton (d. 1958). On 23 June 1959, Spruit founded a new denomination, calling it the "Church of Antioch, Malabar Rite" to signifying its historical connection with those bishops of the Eastern Church who had consecrated Vilatte. In 1965, Spruit took over as primate of the American Catholic Church (Lines Succession), whose history extended back to Vilatte's original American Catholic Church.[150]

The Catholic Apostolic Church of Antioch—Malabar Rite is now based in Santa Fe, New Mexico, and is headed by Archbishop Richard Gundrey (who was appointed by Spruit's widow, Archbishop Meri Spruit). Activities sponsored by the Church and its numerous affiliate churches include a public Sunday mass held at the historic Loretto Chapel in Santa Fe as well as an annual convocation of clergy. The Church of Antioch still exists almost 50 years after its founding and has given rise to numerous other IC denominations, including the New Order of Glastonbury (founded by the late Bishop Martha Shultz), Friends Catholic Communion, and Grace Catholic ("Apostolic Succession") Church.[151]

Conclusion

Initially, this book was penned as a dissertation to satisfy the requirements of a doctorate in theological education from the Graduate Theological Foundation. Its immediate purpose was to provide an updated and more impartial history of esoteric Independent Catholicism for those studying for orders within an IC community. It is of course reasonable to ask, "What is the usefulness of such a history?" In answer, those for whom history is a passion will probably enjoy the foregoing for its own sake. Moreover, I hold that it is important for Independent Catholic parishioners and clergy alike to have some sense of the history of the IC movement.

As I see it, Independent Catholics need to depart from the tendency to define Independent Catholicism primarily in relation to the Roman Catholic Church. Independent Catholicism is a cohesive tradition with a discrete history; those of us who are part of the tradition need to be interested in and continuing to examine its history as honestly as possible. In this way, without obfuscating the controversial elements of Independent Catholicism, we will be able to discuss our tradition intelligently with others. We have an opportunity to speak about Independent Catholic history to a wide and attentive audience—let us do so from an informed and ever-exploring frame of mind.

At this time, at least in the United States, liberal Independent Catholicism has garnered considerable attention from those who seek a spiritual path that is at once sacramental and inclusive. I hope this small offering is just one of many books on the IC tradition that will be available in the coming years. There is much more research and writing to be done on this topic, especially in regard to esoteric Independent Catholicism in the contemporary United States, and many readers interested in pursuing further studies in this area. I strongly encourage those among you who are so inclined to research the lineage and publish your findings.

Notes

INTRODUCTION

1   Peter Frederick Anson, *Bishops at Large* (New York: October House, 1965). While Anson's scholarship is generally solid, his derisive attitude toward independent prelates and churches detracts from the book. The original edition is out of print, and has been recently reprinted by Apocryphile Press (www.apocryphile.org).

2   John P. Plummer, *The Many Paths of the Independent Sacramental Movement* (Dallas Newt Books, 2005), 1-3.

3   For more information on the Independent Anglicans and the Independent Orthodox, see Plummer, *The Many Paths of the Independent Sacramental Movement.*

4   The Catholic Apostolic National Church, *http://www.oldcatholic.com;* the Old Catholic Communion

in North America, http://occna.org/; and the Polish National Catholic Church, http://www.pncc.org.

5   Liberal Catholic Church has various branches, each with its own website; Ecclesia Gnostica, http://www.gnosis.org/eghome.htm; Spiritus Christi, http://www.spirituschristi.org; and Light of Christ Ecumenical Catholic Community, http://www.lightofchristecc.org/.

6   Society of St. Pius V, http://www.sspv.net/ and Society of St. Pius X, http://www.sspx.org/.

7   Theurgy is the practice of rituals designed to invoke gods or planetary spirits for the purpose of achieving spiritual advancement and unification with the divine.

CHAPTER ONE

1   *Apostolic Succession*, n.d., Catholic Answers, Available: http://www.catholic-forum.com/saints/ncd0068 7.htm, 29 March 2006.

2   The historical apostolic succession differs from the history of charismata in the Church. All classes of Christians, not just those who were clergy or leaders, received charismata, such as healing, prophesying, glossalalia, and visions. Dutch scholar Martien Parmentier points out, though, that this seems to shift by the fourth century: "In the Latin West, but also in the Greek East and then also with the Syrians, where once were very many special charismatics, the Church's ministry began to monopolize the charisms. This never worked altogether,

for there were always holy spoilsports who had to be hedged in ecclesiastically, or denounced as heretics. But it is a fact that already in the fourth century at least Western fathers have no doubt that charisms belong with the ministers and not with the lay people." Martien Parmentier, *Water Baptism and Spirit Baptism in the Church Fathers*, 1998, Available: *http://www.pctii.org/cyberj/cyber3.html*, 2 January 2008.

3   Plummer, *The Many Paths of the Independent Sacramental Movement*, 36

4   Email to Siobhán Houston, 10 December 2006.

5   The Roman Catholic Church accepts the Augustinian theory of sacramental validity. Brandreth succinctly explains it thus: "According to this theory a bishop who has been validly consecrated does, when excommunicated or otherwise cut off from the Church, retain [sic] the power of transmitting a succession of valid, if, irregular Orders.... The Augustinian is compelled, therefore, to go on to distinguish between the power conferred in ordination and consecration, and the legitimate exercise of that power." Henry Brandreth, *Episcopi Vagantes and the Anglican Church* (London: Society for Promoting Christian Knowledge, 1947) 6-7. Contemporary ISC bishops and priests may hold valid orders under this definition, but are in an irregular or illicit status, according to Rome, because their ordinations and/or their exercise of their orders occurred without Roman Catholic sanction.

6   Ultramontanists hold that the Pope is God's supreme representative on Earth, in both matters of spir-

it and state. See Richard D. E. Burton, *Blood in the City: Violence and Revelation in Paris, 1789-1954* (Ithaca: Cornell University Press, 2001).

7   Gallicanism maintains that the Pope exerts spiritual but not temporal authority over the French Catholic Church, and should not be involved in matters of state. See Peter Robert Campbell, *Power and Politics in Old Regime France, 1720-1745* (London: Routledge, 1996).

8   Simon Schama, *The Embarrassment of Riches: An Interpretation of Dutch Culture in the Golden Age* (New York: Knopf, 1987), 59.

9   The Port-Royalists under St. Cyran did not refer to themselves as "Jansenists." In fact, they disliked the term and denied its accuracy. The name, though, became synonymous with the centre at Port-Royal and is used by historians to describe that Catholic movement.

10   The Spanish Netherlands were the southern provinces of the Low Countries (including Flanders and the duchy of Luxembourg) that were ruled by Spain or under the sphere of influence of Spain from the mid-sixteenth century until 1713. See Jonathan Israel, *The Dutch Republic: Its Rise, Greatness, and Fall, 1477-1806.* (Oxford: Clarendon Press, 1995).

11   The University of Louvain, now in Belgium, was located in the Spanish Netherlands at this time.

12   *Catholic Encyclopedia, Jansenius and Jansenism,* 1913, Available: *http://www.newadvent.org/cathen/08285a.htm,* 3 January 2008.

13 Claude Beaufor: Moss, *The Old Catholic Movement, Its Origins and History...Second Edition* (London: S.P.C.K, 1964), 34.

14 William Doyle, *Jansenism: Catholic Resistance to Authority from the Reformation to the French Revolution*, Studies in European History (Basingstoke: Macmillan, 2000), 1.

15 Mère Angélique had nineteen brothers and sisters.

16 *Catholic Encyclopedia, Arnauld*, 1913, Available: *http://www.newadvent.org/cathen/01742a.htm*, 4 January 2008.

17 Karl Pruter and J. Gordon Melton, *The Old Catholic Sourcebook* (New York: Garland, 1983), 6.

18 *Catholic Encyclopedia, Port-Royal*, 1913, Available: *http://www.newadvent.org/cathen/12295a.htm*, 3 January 2008.

19 John McManners, *Church and Society in Eighteenth-Century France*, vol. 2, 2 vols (Oxford: Clarendon Press, 1998), 253-54.

20 McManners, *Church and Society in Eighteenth-Century France,* 351.

21 Henry IV was assassinated in 1610.

22 Augustine's critics note that he does not address the role of human free will and the necessity of virtuous living. The Council of Trent (1545-1563) declared that grace

is not attained by faith alone (per Luther). Rather, reconfirming Aquinas's theology, it maintained that grace comes from sacraments and good works. A papal decree in 1625 ended any further debate on the issue of grace. However, this decree was not disseminated in the Spanish Netherlands, where the University of Louvain was located at that time. The University therefore did not formally acknowledge the decree. Doyle, *Jansenism: Catholic Resistance to Authority from the Reformation to the French Revolution,* 5-11.

23   Robin Briggs, *Communities of Belief: Cultural and Social Tension in Early Modern France* (Oxford: Oxford University Press, 1989), 339-42.

24   The Council of Trent (1545-1563) supported the Jesuit view against Luther's declaration of *solo fides.* Doyle, *Jansenism: Catholic Resistance to Authority from the Reformation to the French Revolution,* 5-6.

25   *Catholic Encyclopedia, Port-Royal.*

26   Anne Geneviève de Bourbon-Condé Longueville, b. 1619.

27   William Doyle, *The Old European Order, 1660-1800* (Oxford: Oxford University Press, 1992) 168. For a history of Jansenism more sympathetic to the Jesuits, see Dale van Kley, *The Jansenists and the Expulsion of the Jesuits from France, 1757-1765* (New Haven: Yale University Press, 1975).

28   John McManners, *The Oxford Illustrated History of*

Christianity (Oxford: Oxford University Press, 1990), 271.

29   Pruter and Melton, *The Old Catholic Sourcebook*, 6.

30   Moss, *The Old Catholic Movement, Its Origins and History... Second Edition*, 102.

31   Moss, *The Old Catholic Movement, Its Origins and History... Second Edition*, 106-08.

32   Doyle, *Jansenism: Catholic Resistance to Authority from the Reformation to the French Revolution*, 38-40, 43.

33   McManners, *Church and Society in Eighteenth-Century France* 377. McManners, *The Oxford Illustrated History of Christianity*, 291.

34   Dietrich Blaufuss, "Pietism," *Dictionary of Gnosis and Western Esotericism*, ed. Wouter J. Hanegraaff, vol. 2 (Leiden: Brill, 2005), 956.

35   Peter C. Erb, *Pietists: Selected Writings* (New York: Paulist Press, 1983), 14.

36   Ronald R. Feuerhahn, *The Roots and Fruits of Pietism*, 1998, Concordia Historical Institute and the Luther Academy, Available: *http://www.mtio.com/articles/aissar3.htm*, 31 December 2007.

37   Dianne Guenin-Lelle, *Friends' Theological Heritage: From Seventeenth-Century Quietists to a Guide to True Peace*, 2002, Available: *http://www.quaker.org/quest/issue6-contents.html*, 31 December 2003.

38   Leslek Kolakowski, "Quietism," *Encyclopedia of*

Religion, ed. Lindsay Jones, 2nd ed. (Detroit: Macmillan Reference USA, 2005) 7557-59.

39   Peter George Wallace, *The Long European Reformation: Religion, Political Conflict, and the Search for Conformity, 1350-1750* (New York: Palgrave Macmillan, 2003), 209-10.

40   Kolakowski, "Quietism," 7559.

41   Pruter and Melton, *The Old Catholic Sourcebook*, 6.

42   Moss, *The Old Catholic Movement, Its Origins and History...Second Edition*, 119.

43   Moss, *The Old Catholic Movement, Its Origins and History...Second Edition*, 119-20.

44   Pruter and Melton, *The Old Catholic Sourcebook*, 7.

45   Moss, *The Old Catholic Movement, Its Origins and History...Second Edition*, 122.

46   *Catholic Encyclopedia, Archdiocese of Utrecht*, 1913, Available: *http://www.newadvent.org/cathen/15245a.htm*, 1 January 2008 2007.

47   Moss, *The Old Catholic Movement, Its Origins and History...Second Edition*, 126.

48   Pruter and Melton, *The Old Catholic Sourcebook*, 8.

49   Pruter and Melton, *The Old Catholic Sourcebook*, 13.

50   Moss, *The Old Catholic Movement, Its Origins and History...Second Edition*, 227.

51   Phillip Schaff, *Creeds of Christendom, with a History and Critical Notes (Sixth Edition)*, vol. 1, 3 vols. (1919), 192.

52   Moss, *The Old Catholic Movement, Its Origins and History...Second Edition*, 289.

53   Arthur Carl Piepkorn, *Profiles in Belief: The Religious Bodies of the United States and Canada* (New York: Harper & Row, 1977), 279.

CHAPTER TWO

1   Roger Magraw, *France, 1800-1914 : A Social History* (London ; New York: Longman, 2002), 159-60.

2   Joan Lenardon, *The Civil Constitution of the Clergy as Seen by the Journal Encyclopédique*, 1972, Canadian Catholic Historical Association, Available: *http://www.u manitoba.ca/colleges/st_pauls/ccha/Back%20Issues/CCHA197 2/Lenardon.html*, 4 January 2008.

3   Magraw, *France, 1800-1914 : A Social History*, 162.

4   *Catholic Encyclopedia, the French Concordat of 1801*, 1913, Available: *http://www.newadvent.org/cathen/04204 a.htm*, 6 January 2008.

5   *Catholic Encyclopedia, Schism*, 1913, Available: *http://www.newadvent.org/cathen/13529a.htm*, 2 January 2008.

6   Anson, *Bishops at Large* 299-300. *Catholic Encyclopedia, Schism*. See also Micheal [sic] Thompson, "More Catholic Than the Pope? Varieties of 'Schism' in the Catholic Church in France, 1800-2000," *Comparative Culture: The Journal of Miyazaki International College* 10 (2004). At the time of Anson's research in the 1950s, he reports that there were about 3,500 members of various streams of the *Petite Église*. A French church, *La Petite Église Apostolique Vieille Catholique* (The Little Apostolic Old Catholic Church) claims to be a modern form of the *Petite Église*. See http://users.skynet.be/la.mission/petite _eglise.htm. Another French web site lists an association of several churches in France and Belgium as the inheritors of the *Petite Église*. According to this web site, the association has eight bishops and 324 priests and deacons. See http://www.quid.fr/2007/Religions/Petite_ Eglise/1

7   Anson, *Bishops at Large,* 91.

8   Serge A. Thériault, *Msgr. René Vilatte: Community Organizer of Religion, 1854-1929*, 2nd ed. (Berkeley: Apocryphile Press, 2006), 43-45.

9   Thériault, *Msgr. René Vilatte: Community Organizer of Religion, 1854-1929,* 43-46, 50-51, 57.

10   Thériault, *Msgr. René Vilatte: Community Organizer of Religion, 1854-1929,* 52-54.

11   Thériault, *Msgr. René Vilatte: Community Organizer of Religion, 1854-1929,* 56-57. Anson, *Bishops at Large,* 91-93.

12   Leah Kemp, *Shepherd or Wolf? Joseph René Vilatte in Francophone Wisconsin*, 2001. University of Wisconsin, Available: *http://www.uwgb.edu/~visfrench/study/old_catholics /old_catholics.htm*, 15 December 2007.

13   Anson, *Bishops at Large*, 93-97; Theriault, *Msgr. Rene Vilatte: Community Organizer of Religion, 1854-1929*, 67-72.

14   Theriault, *Msgr. Rene Vilatte: Community Organizer of Religion, 1854-1929* 50-51, 87.

15   Charles Grafton, who became bishop of the Fond du Lac diocese after Brown's death in 1888, wrote a book titled, *The Lineage of the American Catholic Church, Commonly Called the Episcopal Church*. Charles Chapman Grafton, *The Lineage of the American Catholic Church, Commonly Called the Episcopal Church* (Milwaukee, WI: The Young Churchman Company, 1911).

16   Brandreth, *Episcopi Vagantes and the Anglican Church* 95. In 1931, the Old Catholic Church and the Anglican Church entered into full communion.

17   Conversation with Bishop Alexis Tancibok, 11 January 2006.

18   Theriault, *Msgr. Rene Vilatte: Community Organizer of Religion, 1854-1929*, 90-94.

19   Charles Chapman Grafton, *A Journey Godward of [a Servant of Jesus Christ]* (Milwaukee: Young Churchman Co., 1910) 170-72. William M. Hogue, "The Episcopal Church and Archbishop Vilatte," *Historical Magazine of the Protestant Episcopal Church* XXXIV.1 (1965).

20   Theriault, *Msgr. Rene Vilatte: Community Organizer of Religion, 1854-1929,* 107-08.

21   Grafton, *A Journey Godward of [a Servant of Jesus Christ]* 170-71, Hogue, "The Episcopal Church and Archbishop Vilatte," 55.

22   Donald Pierce Weeks, *Joseph Rene Vilatte: First Independent Catholic Prelate in North America,* n.d., Available: *http://www.concentric.net/~Cosmas/vilatte.htm,* 31 December 2007.

23   Moss, *The Old Catholic Movement, Its Origins and History...Second Edition,* 291.

24   Statute 2 from Joseph Rene Vilatte, *Chivalrous & Religious Order of the Crown of Thorns Statutes* (Fort Howard, WI: James Kerr & Son, 1893). Quoted in Theriault, *Msgr. Rene Vilatte: Community Organizer of Religion, 1854-1929* 123. All four of the CCRCC bishops, beginning with Vilatte and including the present bishop, Serge A. Thériault, have been Grand Masters of the OCT. See Theriault, *Msgr. Rene Vilatte: Community Organizer of Religion, 1854-1929* 122-28. Msgr. Serge A. Thériault, *Gaston J. Fercken, 1855-1930,* Available: http://www.ccrcc. ca/documents/gjfercken.pdf, 16 February 2007.

25   Theriault, *Msgr. Rene Vilatte: Community Organizer of Religion, 1854-1929,* 153.

26   Theriault, *Msgr. Rene Vilatte: Community Organizer of Religion, 1854-1929,* 166-67.

27   Even Vilatte's date of death is in dispute. Theriault, *Msgr. Rene Vilatte: Community Organizer of Religion, 1854-1929,* 204. Anson records the date as 8 July 1929. Anson, *Bishops at Large,* 128.

28   Theriault, *Msgr. Rene Vilatte: Community Organizer of Religion, 1854-1929,* 197-204. Hogue, "The Episcopal Church and Archbishop Vilatte," 55.

29   Christian Catholic Church Canada, *Most Reverend J. René Vilatte (1854-1929),* n.d., Christian Catholic Church Canada, Available: *http://cccc.ca/en/episcopal_committee/cccc/mem_jr_vilatte.html* 28 December 2007. Referencing Bernard Vignot, *Les Églises Parallèles* (Paris: Cerf, 1991), 36.

30   Anson, *Bishops at Large,* 128.

31   For more information on this schism, see Anson, *Bishops at Large,* 105.

32   "As a note on Fabré-Palaprat's church, they did not call it the *"Église Johannite des Chrétiens Primitifs,"* in the ordination rituals, and on the certificates of ordination is it referred to as either *"la Sainte Église du Christ"* or the *"Église Chrétienne."* Phillip Garver (Tau Vincent II), email to Siobhán Houston, 25 June 2008.

33   Anson, *Bishops at Large,* 300-01.

34   Phillip A. Garver, *The History of the Gnostic Church, 2001-2006,* Available: *http://www.plerome.org/histoire.htm,* 3 January 2008.

35   Anson, *Bishops at Large,* 300-02.

36   A Greek term for the Holy Spirit, meaning "comforter."

37   Burton, *Blood in the City: Violence and Revelation in Paris, 1789-1954,* 163-65.

38   Judith Devlin, *The Superstitious Mind: French Peasants and the Supernatural in the Nineteenth Century* (New Haven: Yale University Press, 1987) 150-51. For more on Naundorff's royalist claim, see Anna Meyer, *Hunting the Double Helix: How DNA Is Solving Puzzles of the Past* (Crows Nest, NSW, Australia: Allen & Unwin, 2005), 180-92.

39   Anson, *Bishops at Large,* 302-03.

40   Anson, *Bishops at Large,* 302-03.

41   Anson, *Bishops at Large,* 303-04.

42   Christopher McIntosh, *Eliphas Lévi and the French Occult Revival* (London: Rider and Company, 1972), 116.

43   Anson spells his name *Charuoz.*

44   McIntosh, *Eliphas Lévi and the French Occult Revival,* 107-10.

45   McIntosh, *Eliphas Lévi and the French Occult Revival* 179-89. Anson, *Bishops at Large* 304. Burton, *Blood in the City: Violence and Revelation in Paris, 1789-1954* 162-66. J.K. Huysman's novel, *La-Bas,* is set in the occult under-

ground in France and features a character modeled after Abbé Boullan.

46   Raymond Rudorff, *The Belle Epoque* (New York: Saturday Review Press, 1973), 193.

47   Pope Leo VIII *Humanum Genus*, 1884, Available: *http://www.papalencyclicals.net/Leo13/l13human.htm*, 2 January 2008.

48   Richard Smoley, *Inner Christianity: A Guide to the Esoteric Tradition* (Boston: Shambhala, 2002), 36. See also McIntosh, *Eliphas Lévi and the French Occult Revival*.

49   Ladislaus Toth, "Gnostic Church," *Dictionary of Gnosis and Western Esotericism*, ed. Wouter J. Hanegraaff, vol. I (Leiden: Brill, 2001), 400.

50   Plummer, *The Many Paths of the Independent Sacramental Movement,* 32.

51   Tau is an honorific for modern Gnostic elders.

52   Gnostic teacher whose movement flourished c. 100 CE.

53   Synesius, *L'arbre Gnostique* (Paris: Chamuel, 1899), 67.

54   Marie, Countess of Caithness, a Roman Catholic and an important figure in esoteric and spiritualist circles in Paris, was the president of the first Theosophical Society chapter in France, established 28 June 1883. Joscelyn Godwin, *The Beginnings of Theosophy in France*

(London: Theosophical History Centre, 1989) 9. See also Joscelyn Godwin, "Lady Caithness and Her Connection with Theosophy," *Theosophical History* VIII.4 (2000).

55   Garver, *The History of the Gnostic Church*. For an explanation of the Greek terms of the early Christian Gnostics, see Elaine Pagels, *The Gnostic Gospels* (New York: Random House, 1981). Also see Richard Smoley, *Forbidden Faith: The Gnostic Legacy from the Gospels to the Da Vinci Code* (San Francisco: HarperSanFrancisco, 2006). Marvin Meyer and James M. Robinson, *The Nag Hammadi Scriptures* (San Francisco: HarperOne, 2007).

56   The Paulicians were a dualistic Christian sect that probably originated in sixth-century Armenia. See J.M. Hussey, *The Orthodox Church in the Byzantine Empire* (Oxford: Clarendon, 1990), 156-60.

57   Edina Bozoky, "Catharism," *Dictionary of Gnosis and Western Esotericism*, ed. Wouter J. Hanegraaff, vol. 1 (Leiden: Brill, 2005), 244-45.

58   Malcolm Lambert, *The Cathars* (Oxford: Blackwell, 1998), 33.

59   Lambert, *The Cathars,* 21-22.

60   Bozoky, "Catharism," 245-46. Lambert, *The Cathars,* 21-22, 73-74.

61   The French town of Albi was a Cathar stronghold.

62   Bozoky, "Catharism," 244-45.

63   Interestingly, his teacher, Peter Deunov, sent the Bulgarian Gnostic Christian teacher Omraam Mikhaël Aïvanhov to France in 1937. Leaving behind the Communist repression of his native land, Aivanhov lived and taught in France for fifty years and became well known internationally. He claimed his tradition was connected to the Bogomils.

64   In his essay on Neo-Catharism, Introvigne describes numerous other examples of Neo-Cathar movements, all later than Doinel. Massimo Introvigne, "Neo-Catharism," *Dictionary of Gnosis and Western Esotericism*, ed. Wouter J. Hanegraaff, vol. 2 (Leiden: Brill, 2005), 827-28.

65   The best source for primary documents from the French Gnostic churches is Rene Le Forestier, *L'occultisme En France Aux Xixeme Et Xxeme Siecles: L'église Gnostique*, ed. Antoine Faivre (Milano: Arche, 1990). This book is out of print and extremely rare, so I have included sources for electronic versions of these documents. The most reputable and learned American historian and translator of the work of the French Gnostics is Phillip A. Garver (Tau Vincent II), whose web site is *www.gnostique.net*. Jules Stany Doinel, *The Valentinian Gnosis*, Available: *http://www.gnostique.net/documents/ValGnose.htm*, 31 December 2007. Jules Stany Doinel, *The First Homily: "On the Holy Gnosis,"* 1890, Available: *http://www.gnostique. net/documents/homelie1.htm*, 21 December 2007. See also Introvigne, "Neo-Catharism."

66   Doinel, *The Valentinian Gnosis*.

67   Garver, *The History of the Gnostic Church*.

68   Garver, *The History of the Gnostic Church*.

69   Synesius, *L'arbre Gnostique* 71. Trans. by Phillip Garver. Email to Siobhán Houston, October 26, 2006.

70   Introvigne, "Neo-Catharism," 826.

71   Garver, *The History of the Gnostic Church*. See Jules Stany Doinel, *Rituel De La Fraction Du Pain*, n.d., Available: *http://user.cyberlink.ch/~koenig/pain.htm*,   8 August 2007. See also Pierre Geyraud, *Gnostic Priestess*, Translated by Phillip A. Garver, from *Les Petites Églises De Paris (Parmi Les Sects Et Les Rites)*. Paris: Editions Emile-Paul Frères) 76-83., 1937, Available: *http://www.gnostique. net/documents/pretresse.htm*, 5 January 2008.

72   Jules Stany Doinel, *Le Rituel De L'appareillamentum*, n.d., Available: *http://user.cyberlink.ch/~koenig/appareil.htm*, 12 December 2007.

73   Lambert, *The Cathars*, 142.

74   Rudorff, *The Belle Epoque, 199-205*. See also Arthur Edward Waite, *Devil Worship in France or the Question of Lucifer* (London: George Redway, 1896). Papus wrote a defense against Taxil's work, a pamphlet entitled *Le Diable et L'Occultisme*, which appeared in 1895.

75   Garver, *The History of the Gnostic Church*.

76   Garver, *The History of the Gnostic Church*.

77   Bishop Jean (Tau Jean II) Bricaud, *Patriarchal Homily*, 1908, Trans. by Phillip A. Garver, Available: *http://*

www.gnostique.net/documents/homeliej2.htm, 21 December 2007.

78   Joanny Bricaud, *Profession De Foi*, n.d., Available: *http://user.cyberlink.ch/~koenig/profess.htm*, 12 December 2007. The profession is signed by the Supreme Council of the High Synod, whose members were Bricaud, Fugarion, Jean Baptiste (bishop of Russia), Clement, Bishop of the United States of America, head deacon Marcel Cotte, and head deaconess Houdja Iietzel

79   D. L. L. Parry and Pierre Girard, *France since 1800: Squaring the Hexagon* (Oxford Oxford University Press, 2002) 89. Robert Tombs, *France 1814-1914* (London: Longman, 1996) 456. See also Andrew Sedgewick, *The Raillement in French Politics, 1890-1898* (Cambridge: Harvard University Press), 1965.

80   Tombs, *France 1814-1914*. 468.

81   Parry and Girard, *France since 1800: Squaring the Hexagon*, 99.

82   Tombs, *France 1814-1914* 468, "Gnostics Still a Church: With 250 Members in the World—Head in France a Bookkeeper," *New York Times*, 27 November 1910.

83   Parry and Girard, *France since 1800: Squaring the Hexagon*, 99-101.

84   Magraw, *France, 1800-1914 : A Social History*, 176.

85   Anson, *Bishops at Large*, 122-23, 305.

86   Anson, *Bishops at Large,* 120.

87   Many of Abbe Julio's books have been reprinted recently by Editions Bussière. *http://www.editionsbussiere.com*

88   Anson, *Bishops at Large,* 307-08.

89   "Martinezist" is used to describe those who follow Martinez de Pasqually's theurgical path, to differentiate them from Martinists who follow Saint-Martin's more contemplative way.

90   Antoine Faivre defines theosophy generally as "a gnosis that has a bearing not only on the salvific relations the individual maintains with the divine world, but also on the nature of God Himself, or of divine persons, and on the natural universe, the origin of that universe, the hidden structures that constitute it in its actual state, its relationship to mankind, and its final ends." Antoine Faivre, *Access to Western Esotericism* (Albany: State University of New York Press, 1994), 23.

91   Serge Caillet, *Martinism Today,* 2000, Available: *http://www.france-spiritualites.fr/interview-serge-caillet-martinism-today.htm*, 30 December 2007.

92   McIntosh, *Eliphas Lévi and the French Occult Revival* 20-25. For a detailed explication of Pasqually's history and teachings, see Rene Le Forestier, Antoine Faivre and Alec Mellor, *La Franc-Maconnerie Templiere Et Occultiste Aux Xviiie Et Xixe Siecles* (Paris: La Table d'emeraude, 1987) Tome 1, 290-313.

93   Faivre, *Access tc Westerr. Esotericism,* 73.

94   Robert (Sar Aurifer) Ambelain, *The Martinist Doctrine*, n.d., Available: *uttp://www.ancientmartinist order.org/Aurifer.htm,* 28 November 2007.

95   Jesus Christ is also known as the Active and Intelligent Cause or the Redeemer in Pasqually's and Saint-Martin's philosophy.

96   Arthur Edward Waite, *The Unknown Philosopher: The Life of Louis Claude De St. Martin and the Substance of His Transcendental Doctrine* (Montana, USA: Kessinger Publishing Company, n.d.), 36-38.

97   McIntosh, *Eliphas Lévi and the French Occult Revival,* 18-19, 40-41.

98   Jean-Francois Var, "Martines De Pasqually," *Dictionary of Gnosis and Western Esotericism*, ed. Wouter J. Hanegraaff, vol. 2 (Leiden: Brill, 2005), 933.

99   "Sar" is a title of Assyrian royalty that is used as an honorific for Martinist masters. Rudorff, *The Belle Epoque,* 188.

100   Caillet, *Martinism Today*.

101   Faivre, *Access to Western Esotericism,* 73.

102   Arthur McCalla, "Louis-Claude De Saint-Martin," *Dictionary of Gnosis and Western Esotericism*, ed. Wouter J. Hanegraaff, vol. 2 (2005), 1024-25.

103 Waite, *The Unknown Philosopher: The Life of Louis Claude De St.Martin and the Substance of His Transcendental Doctrine,* 25.

104 Arthur Versluis, "Christian Theosophical Literature of the Seventeenth and Eighteenth Centuries," *Gnosis and Hermeticism: From Antiquity to Modern Times,* eds. Roelef van der Broek and Wouter J. Hanegraaff (Albany: State University Press of New York, 1998), 230.

105 Edward Mazet, "Freemasonry and Esotericism," *Modern Esoteric Spirituality,* eds. Antoine Faivre and Jacob Needleman (London: SCM Press Ltd, 1993), 264-65.

106 Antoine Faivre, "The Notions of Concealment and Secrecy in Modern Esoteric Currents since the Renaissance (a Methodological Approach)," *Rending the Veil: Concealment and Secrecy in the History of Religions,* ed. Elliot R. Wolfson (New York: Seven Bridges Press, 1999), 162.

107 Philippe Encausse, *Papus, Le Balzac De L'occultisme: Vingt-Cinq Annees D'occultisme Occidental* (Paris: Pierre Belfond, 1979), 49.

108 Encausse, *Papus, Le Balzac De L'occultisme: Vingt-Cinq Annees D'occultisme Occidental,* 81.

109 Jean-Pierre Laurant, "The Primitive Characteristics of Nineteenth-Century Esotericism," *Modern Esoteric Spirituality,* eds. Antoine Faivre and Jacob Needleman (London: SCM Press Ltd, 1993), 285.

110 Laurant, "The Primitive Characteristics of Nineteenth-Century Esotericism," 164.

111 Steven M. Wasserstrom, *Religion after Religion: Gershom Scholem, Mircea Eliade, and Henry Corbin at Eranos* (Princeton, N.J.: Princeton University Press, 1999), 44.

112 Encausse, *Papus, Le Balzac De L'occultisme: Vingt-Cinq Annees D'occultisme Occidental*, 50.

113 Colin Wilson, *The Occult* (New York: Random House, 1971), 249.

114 Jean-Pierre Laurant, *L'escterisme Chrétien En France Au Xixe Siecle* (Lausanne: L'Age d'homme, 1992) 165. A 1910 *New York Times* article discusses Bricaud's church, stating that Jean II (Bricaud) is employed as a bookkeeper for a "commercial concern." Bricaud is quoted as being gratified to hear that his church had been accused of heresy by "an organ of the Vatican:" "That proves...that we are feared." "Gnostics Still a Church: With 250 Members in the World—Head in France a Bookkeeper."

115 Massimo Introvigne, "Martinism: Second Period," *Dictionary of Gnosis and Western Esotericism*, ed. Wouter J. Hanegraaff, vol. 2 (Leiden: Brill, 2005), 781.

116 Caillet, *Martinism Today*.

CHAPTER THREE

1   Literally, "wandering bishops," the term loosely refers to independent bishops in general.

2   Brandreth, *Episcopi Vagantes and the Anglican Church*, ix-xiv. Not all scholars agree with Douglas. See Eric A. Badertscher, *The Measure of a Bishop: The Episcopi Vagantes, Apostolic Succession, and the Legitimacy of the Anglican "Continuing Church" Movement*, 1998, Project Canterbury, Available: http://anglicanhistory.org/essays/badertscher/index.html, 4 January 2008.

3   David Morse, *High Victorian Culture* (Houndmills: Macmillan, 1993), 229.

4   The Caroline Divines were a group of Anglican High Church scholars who wished to "recover the simplicity and purity of early Christianity." John R. H. Moorman, *A History of the Church in England* (New York: Morehouse-Gorham, 1954), 233-36.

5   C. Brad Faught, *The Oxford Movement: A Thematic History of the Tractarians and Their Times* (University Park, PA: Pennsylvania State University Press, 2003), 9.

6   W. S. F. Pickering, *Anglo-Catholicism: A Study in Religious Ambiguity* (London: Routledge, 1989), 28.

7   Pickering, *Anglo-Catholicism: A Study in Religious Ambiguity*, 39-49.

8   Pickering, *Anglo-Catholicism: A Study in Religious Ambiguity*, 136, 93.

9   Morse, *High Victorian Culture,* 219.

10   Geoffrey Rowell, *The Vision Glorious: Themes and Personalities of the Catholic Revival in Anglicanism* (Oxford: Oxford University Press, 1983), 4.

11   Faught, *The Oxford Movement: A Thematic History of the Tractarians and Their Times,* 33.

12   Faught, *The Oxford Movement: A Thematic History of the Tractarians and Their Times,* 19.

13   Owen Chadwick, *The Spirit of the Oxford Movement: Tractarian Essays* (Cambridge: Cambridge University Press, 1990), 2.

14   Thomas Ferguson, "The Enthralling Power: History and Heresy in John Henry Newman," *Anglican Theological Review* (2003).

15   Rowell, *The Vision Glorious: Themes and Personalities of the Catholic Revival in Anglicanism,* 2.

16   Richard Tarnas, *The Passion of the Western Mind* (New York: Ballantine Books, 1991), 232.

17   Chadwick, *The Spirit of the Oxford Movement: Tractarian Essays,* 19.

18   Peter A. Kwasniewski, *The Conversion of John Henry Newman,* 1999, Available: *http://www.catholic.net/rcc/ Periodicals/Faith/JAN-FEB99/Conversion.html,* 13 December 2007.

19   Herbert Schlossberg, *Religious Revival and the Transformation of English Sensibilities in the Early Nineteeenth Century*, n.d., Prof. George Landow, Brown University, Available: *http://www.victorianweb.org/religion/intro.html*, 11 December 2007.

20   Arnold Harris Mathew, *An Episcopal Odyssey. An Open Letter to the Archbishop of Canterbury, Etc.* (Kingsdown, 1915), 13.

21   The lesser (or minor) excommunication means that the person may not be offered the sacraments. The greater (or major) excommunication is removal from the church. Minor excommunication is no longer recognized in Catholic canon law. Moss, *The Old Catholic Movement, Its Origins and History... Second Edition,* i.

22   Anson, *Bishops at Large,* 158-63.

23   Mathew, *An Episcopal Odyssey. An Open Letter to the Archbishop of Canterbury, Etc.* 15. Mathew does not specify to which congregation he is referring. In 1892, Rev. Eyton was the Rector of Holy Trinity and in fact officiated at Mathew's wedding that year. In 1895, he was appointed Rector of St Margaret's and Canon of Westminster. Anson, *Bishops at Large,* 162-63.

24   Brandreth, *Episcopi Vagantes and the Anglican Church,* 12.

25   Brandreth, *Episcopi Vagantes and the Anglican Church,* 12.

26   Moss, *The Old Catholic Movement, Its Origins and*

History...Second Edition, 300. This synod was most probably a concoction of O'Halloran's imagination. Anson, *Bishops at Large,* 174.

27   James I. Wedgwood, *The Beginnings of the Liberal Catholic Church,* 1937, Global Library, Available: *http://www.global.org/Pub/JIW_History.asp,* 12 December 2007.

28   Mathew is referring to Rev. Richard O'Halloran.

29   Mathew, *An Episcopal Odyssey. An Open Letter to the Archbishop of Canterbury, Etc.,* 7, 10. Christof Schuler rebuts Mathew's claim that he was duped by O'Halloran. Christoph Schuler, *The Mathew Affair: The Failure to Establish an Old Catholic Church in England in the Context of Anglican Old Catholic Relations between 1902 and 1925* (Amersfoot: Stichting Centraal Oud-Katholiek Boekhuis, 1997).

30   Mathew, *An Episcopal Odyssey. An Open Letter to the Archbishop of Canterbury, Etc.* 21. The declaration was published in *The Guardian* on 6 January 1911.

31   Moss, *The Old Catholic Movement, Its Origins and History... Second Edition,* 304-05.

32   Moss, *The Old Catholic Movement, Its Origins and History... Second Edition,* 300-07.

33   Rev. Anthony Cekada, SSPX, *A Warning on the Old Catholics: False Bishops, False Churches,* 1980, Available: *http://sspx.agenda.tripod.com/id73.html,* 12 December 2007.

34   Mathew, *An Episcopal Odyssey. An Open Letter to the Archbishop of Canterbury, Etc.,* 8-9.

35   His full name was Rudolph Francis Edward St. Patrick Alphonsus Ghislain de Gramont Hamilton de Lorraine-Brabant, Prince de Landas Berghes et de Rache, Duc de St. Winock. *Old Catholic Church, A Short History,* n.d., Old Catholic Church of America, Available: *http://www.oldcatholic.org/history.htm,* 4 January 2008.

36   Willoughby served as an Anglican priest from 1899-1906.

37   Church, *A Short History.* While the clergy and churches in the lines of Carfora and Mickiewicz are central to American Old Catholic history, they are, almost without exception, traditional in doctrine and practice. For more information on these bishops, see Peter Anson, *Bishops at Large.*

38   Anson, *Bishops at Large,* 324.

39   Anson, *Bishops at Large,* 194-95.

40   Anson, *Bishops at Large* 346. Dositheos, the patriarch of Jerusalem, convened the Synod of Jerusalem. The Synod of Jerusalem condemned the work, the *Confession of Faith* (1629), which was heavily influenced by Calvinism.

41   Janet Oppenheim, *The Other World: Spiritualism and Psychical Research in England, 1850-1914* (Cambridge: Cambridge University Press, 1985), 167.

42   Wedgwood, *The Beginnings of the Liberal Catholic Church*.

43   Mathew, *An Episcopal Odyssey. An Open Letter to the Archbishop of Canterbury, Etc.,* 8.

44   Mathew, *An Episcopal Odyssey. An Open Letter to the Archbishop of Canterbury, Etc.,* 6-7.

45   Mathew, *An Episcopal Odyssey. An Open Letter to the Archbishop of Canterbury, Etc.* 8-9, 12-13.

46   Anson, *Bishops at Large,* 204-05.

47   Anson, *Bishops at Large,* 324-40. One church directly tracing their lineage to Williams is the Old Catholic Church of Great Britain. Their web site posits that the Old Catholic Church of England established by Mathew did not become the Liberal Catholic Church but survives as *their* church. *www.oldcatholic.co.ac*

48   For another view of Arnold Harris Mathew and his relations with the Old Catholic Church, see Schuler, *The Mathew Affair: The Failure to Establish an Old Catholic Church in England in the Context of Anglican Old Catholic Relations between 1902 and 1925* (Amerfoot: Stichting Centraal Oud-Katholiek Boekhuis, 1997). This book, written by an Old Catholic priest, is currently out of print and very difficult to find in the States.

49   Nicola Bown, Carolyn Burdett and Pamela Thurschwell, *The Victorian Supernatural*, Cambridge Studies in Nineteenth-Century Literature and Culture; 42 (Cambridge: Cambridge University Press, 2004), 1.

50   Aileen Fyfe and John van Whye, *Victorian Science and Religion*, n.d, Available: *http://www.victorianweb.org/science/science&religion.html*, 12 December 2007.

51   Oppenheim, *The Other World: Spiritualism and Psychical Research in England, 1850-1914*, 1.

52   John Hedley Brooke, *Science and Religion: Some Historical Perspectives*, Cambridge History of Science (Cambridge: Cambridge University Press, 1991), 6-11, 321.

53   See Wouter J. Hanegraaff, *New Age Religion and Western Culture: Esotericism in the Mirror of Secular Thought* (Albany: State University of New York, 1998) 384-444. Frances Amelia Yates, *The Rosicrucian Enlightenment* (Boston: Shambhala, 1978) 220-33. Christopher H. Partridge, *The Re-Enchantment of the West: Alternative Spiritualities, Sacralization, Popular Culture, and Occulture*, 2 vols. (London: T & T Clark International, 2004).

54   Dan Burton and David Grandy, *Magic, Mystery, and Science: The Occult in Western Civilization* (Bloomington: Indiana University Press, 2004), 184.

55   Karl E. Beckson, *London in the 1890s: A Cultural History*, 1st ed. (New York: W.W. Norton, 1992), 317-19.

56   Alex Owen, *The Place of Enchantment: British Occultism and the Culture of the Modern* (Chicago: University of Chicago Press, 2004), 18.

57   Alex Owen, *The Darkened Room: Women, Power and Spiritualism in Late Victorian England* (Philadelphia: University of Pennsylvania Press, 1990) 21, Hanegraaff, *New Age Religion and Western Culture: Esotericism in the Mirror of Secular Thought,* 435.

58   Oppenheim, *The Other World: Spiritualism and Psychical Research in England 1850-1914* 161. See also Richard Noakes, "Spiritualism, Science and the Supernatural in Mid-Victorian Britain," *The Victorian Supernatural,* eds. Nicola Bown, Carolyn Burdett and Pamela Thurschwell, Cambridge Studies in Nineteenth-Century Literature and Culture: 42 (Cambridge, UK: Cambridge University Press, 2004).

59   Oppenheim, *The Other World: Spiritualism and Psychical Research in England, 1850-1914,* 3.

60   Burton and Grandy, *Magic, Mystery, and Science: The Occult in Western Civilization,* 185.

61   Burton and Grandy, *Magic, Mystery, and Science: The Occult in Western Civilization.* 184.

62   Oppenheim, *The Other World: Spiritualism and Psychical Research in England, 1850-1914,* 2.

63   Owen, *The Place of Enchantment: British Occultism and the Culture of the Modern,* 4-7.

64   Oppenheim *The Other World: Spiritualism and Psychical Research in England, 1850-1914,* 164.

65   Alison Butler, "Magical Beginnings: The Intellectual Origins of the Victorian Occult Revival," *Limina: A Journal of Historical and Cultural Studies* 9 (2003).

66   Owen, *The Place of Enchantment: British Occultism and the Culture of the Modern,* 8-15.

67   Faivre, *Access to Western Esotericism,* 88.

68   W. Michael Ashcraft, *The Dawn of the New Cycle: Point Loma Theosophists and American Culture,* 1st ed. (Knoxville: University of Tennessee Press, 2002), 3.

69   Owen, *The Place of Enchantment: British Occultism and the Culture of the Modern,* 28-34.

70   Joy Dixon, *Divine Feminine: Theosophy and Feminism in England* (Baltimore: Johns Hopkins University Press, 2001), 3.

71   Owen, *The Place of Enchantment: British Occultism and the Culture of the Modern,* 24.

72   Dixon, *Divine Feminine: Theosophy and Feminism in England,* 3-8.

73   Diana Basham, *The Trial of Woman: Feminism and the Occult Sciences in Victorian Literature and Society* (Houndmills: Macmillan, 1992) 203-04. See also Lenore Davidoff, "Class and Gender in Victorian England," *Sex and Class in Women's History*, eds. Judith Lowder Newton, Mary P. Ryan and Judith R. Walkowitz (London: Routledge and Kegan Paul, 1983), Philippa Levine, *Feminist Lives in Victorian England: Private Roles and Public*

Commitment (Oxford: B. Blackwell, 1990), Joan Perkin, *Victorian Women* (London: J Murray, 1993), Frank M. Turner, *Contesting Cultural Authority: Essays in Victorian Intellectual Life* (Cambridge: Cambridge University Press, 1993).

74   Independent and Rectified Order R.R. et A.C. was founded in November 1903.

75   Owen, *The Place of Enchantment: British Occultism and the Culture of the Modern* 48-49. For more information on Underhill's work with Waite, see R.A. Gilbert, *A.E. Waite: Magician of Many Parts* (Kent, UK: Aquarian Press, 1987).

76   Collected Writings, 1950, vol. XI, 414. Quoted in Joscelyn Godwin, *The Theosophical Enlightenment* (Albany: State University of New York Press, 1994), 328.

77   Oppenheim, *The Other World: Spiritualism and Psychical Research in England, 1850-1914,* 187.

78   Godwin, *The Theosophical Enlightenment,* 333-42.

79   Godwin, *The Theosophical Enlightenment* 342-46. See Nicholas Goodrick-Clarke, "Hermeticism and Hermetic Societies," *Dictionary of Gnosis and Western Esotericism,* ed. Wouter J. Hanegraaff, vol. 1 (Leiden: Brill, 2005) 552-55. See also Alan Pert, *Red Cactus: The Life of Anna Kingsford,* 2nd. ed. (NSW, Australia: Books and Writers 2007).

80   Dixon, *Divine Feminine: Theosophy and Feminism in England,* 74-75.

81   Godwin, *The Theosophical Enlightenment,* 367.

82   Wedgwood, *The Beginnings of the Liberal Catholic Church.*

83   Walter Walsh, *The Secret History of the Oxford Movement* (London: Swan Sonnenschein, 1897).

84   Quoted in Maurice Warnon, *Biography [of James Ingall Wedgwood],* n.d., Liberal Catholic Church, Available: *http://kingsgarden.org/English/Organizations/LCC.gb/LCIS/Sc riptures/Liberal/Wedgwood/WedgwoodBiography.html,*   4 January 2008. While the Confraternity is extant, it almost ceased to exist soon after its inception due to the fact that many of its members joined the Roman Catholic Church went over to Rome. "Its main aim was to inculcate fasting before holy communion and the practice of confession." Pickering, *Anglo-Catholicism: A Study in Religious Ambiguity,* 45.

85   Anson, *Bishops at Large,* 345.

86   Universal Co-Masonry, which had its origins in France in 1893, was transmitted to the UK in 1902 through the TS. Besant and Leadbeater became very involved with this type of Freemasonry that admits both men and women.

87   Wedgwood, *The Beginnings of the Liberal Catholic Church.*

88   Anson, *Bishops at Large,* 345.

89   Wedgwood, *The Beginnings of the Liberal Catholic Church.*

90   Archbishop Mathew publicly charged that Wedgwood's consecration was invalid because Willoughby, a bishop suspended by Mathew, carried out the consecration. Bruce F. Campbell, *Ancient Wisdom Revised: A History of the Theosophical Movement* (Berkeley: University of California Press, 1980), 126.

91   Geoffrey Hodson, *Introduction*, n.d. [c. 1965], Available: *http://www.alpheus.org/html/articles/theosophy/oncwl1.html#t1*, 4 January 2008.

92   Gregory Tillett, *The Elder Brother* (London: Routledge & Kegan Paul Books, Ltd., 1982), 18.

93   Tillett, *The Elder Brother.* 187-90.

94   Martyn became instrumental in the "Back to Blavatsky" movement, setting up a TS Loyalty League in Sydney. Charles Webster Leadbeater, James I. Wedgwood and Annie Besant, *Occultism of the Mass and the Old Catholic Church Movement. A Collection of Essays from Writings and Documents.* (Krotona: Theosophical Publishing House, 1918).

95   Andrew Prescott, *'Builders of the Temple of the New Civilisation': Annie Besant and Freemasonry*, n.d., University of Sheffield Centre for Research into Freemasonry, Available: *http://freemasonry.dept.shef.ac.uk/pdf/besant.pdf* 1 December 2007.

96   Kevin Tingay, "The Ritual Dimension of Theosophy: Some Forgotten Endeavours," *Theosophical History* X.3 (July 2004).

97   Tillett, *The Elder Brother* 161. See also Tillett, *The Elder Brother,* 117.

98   Charles J. Ryan, *H. P. Blavatsky and the Theosophical Movement* (Pasadena, CA: Theosophical University Press, 1975), Chapter 23.

99   Wedgwood, *The Beginnings of the Liberal Catholic Church*.

100   Tillett, *The Elder Brother,* 173.

101   Wedgwood, *The Beginnings of the Liberal Catholic Church*.

102   An exact copy of the original missal has been published and is available from Apocryphile Press (www.apocryphile.org).

103   Wedgwood, *The Beginnings of the Liberal Catholic Church*. St. Alban, one of the early incarnations of the Count, is the patron saint of the LCC. St. Alban is the first known martyr of the British church, who was tortured and beheaded in c. 209 during the rule of Emperor Septimius Severus. His biography in the June 1925 issue of *The Liberal Catholic* details an expanded understanding of the saint's seminal role in western civilization as informed by the concealed stream of history: "A great Saint, a great Philosopher, a great Statesman, a great Scientist, a Teacher and a Hierophant of Divine Mysteries,

a great Poet and a great Soldier—all these has the Master [St. Alban] been during his many lives in Europe, and He shows forth the complexity of the Seventh Ray of which he is the Head, its worldliness and otherworldliness, its synthesis of art and science, of religious devotion and of ability to govern." James A. Santucci, "Theosophical Society," *Dictionary of Gnosis and Western Esotericism*, ed. Wouter J. Hanegraaff, vol. 2 (Leiden: Brill, 2005) 1121.

104 James I. Wedgwood, *The Presence of Christ in the Holy Communion and Other Writings* (London: St Alban's Press, 1984), 3.

105 Leadbeater, Wedgwood and Besant, *Occultism of the Mass and the Old Catholic Church Movement. A Collection of Essays from Writings and Documents*, 90.

106 Warren Christopher Platt, "The Liberal Catholic Church: An Analysis of a Hybrid Sect." Dissertation, Columbia University 1982, 45-46.

107 *Catholic Encyclopedia, Apocatastasis*, 1913, Available: *http://www.newadvent.org/cathen/01599a.htm*, 8 January 2008.

108 The LCC is governed by its General Episcopal Synod, which is comprised of all LCC bishops and is headed by the Presiding Bishop. The first synod took place in August 1916 under the charge of James Wedgwood. Platt, "The Liberal Catholic Church: An Analysis of a Hybrid Sect," 45-46.

109 Wedgwood, *The Presence of Christ in the Holy Communion and Other Writings,* xii-xiii.

110 Theosophy holds that each human is comprised of seven interpenetrating "sheaths" or bodies ranging from the physical body, the most gross, to the mental body, which is the subtlest.

111 The eleventh edition of the book runs to 630 pages.

112 Charles Webster Leadbeater, "Hidden Side of Christian Festivals," *The Liberal Catholic* II.1 (1925).

113 "Bishop Wedgwood used to say that...the best contribution the worshipper can make is to pour out devotion and thought at the highest possible level during the Eucharist and leave the building of the Form to the angels." "An Appreciation by the Rev. G.N. Drinkwater" in Godwin, *The Theosophical Enlightenment* 368. See also Charles Webster Leadbeater, *The Science of the Sacraments*, Eleventh reprint ed. (Adyar: Theosophical Publishing House, 1999).

114 Godwin, *The Theosophical Enlightenment,* 368.

115 Leadbeater, *The Science of the Sacraments,* 299-308.

116 An excellent resource on the LCC is Platt, "The Liberal Catholic Church: An Analysis of a Hybrid Sect."

117 Whalen, William Joseph. *Separated Brethren; a Survey of Non-Catholic Christian Denominations in the United States* (Milwaukee: Bruce Pub. Co., 1958), 210.

118 Charles Webster Leadbeater, *The Masters and the Path*, 1940 (1st ed. 1925), Anand Golap, Available: *http://www.anandgholap.net/Masters_And_Path-CWL.htm*, 1 December 2007. "In Theosophical parlance, Devaloka is the heavenly realm. Devachan is the heavenly realm; Kamaloca is purgatory; Deva-loka (only one instance of this in HPB's work) is the abode of the gods or Devas in the six superior spheres above Mount Meru. Godwin may have confused the first two terms." Personal communication from Dr. Nicholas Goodrick-Clarke to Siobhán Houston, 2007.

119 This new human group would be the sixth sub-race of the fifth Aryan Root-Race. According to Besant, these psychically gifted people would first appear in California, which comes as no surprise to those of us native Californians.

120 E.L. Gardner, *There Is No Religion Higher Than Truth: Developments in the Theosophical Society*, 1963, The Theosophical Publishing House, Ltd., Available: *http://www.theosophical.ca/NoReligion.htm*, 24 December 2007, Leadbeater, *The Masters and the Path*.

121 According to Theosophical tenets, Lord Maitreya is one of the Ascended Masters (perfected beings) who resides in the Himalayas and who direct the evolution of the earth. Lord Maitreya is specifically charged with the task of overseeing religion and education. To this end, he sends emissaries to establish religions and teach universal truths; occasionally he himself incarnates. Lord Maitreya has incarnated twice, according to Leadbeater—using the bodies or "vehicles" of Lord Krishna and of Master Jesus.

Roland Vernon, *Star in the East* (Boulder, CO: Sentient Publications, 2002) 47.

122   E.L. Gardner avers that Charles Webster Leadbeater was the true force behind the World-Teacher movement in the TS. Rudolf Steiner, *The Spiritual Guidance of the Individual and Humanity*, trans. Samuel Desch (Hudson, NY: Anthroposophic Press, 1991), ix.

123   Plummer, *The Many Paths of the Independent Sacramental Movement,* 78-79.

124   Anne Taylor, *Annie Besant: A Biography* (Oxford: Oxford University Press, 1992), 323-234.

125   Johannes Jacobus van der Leeuw, *Revelation or Realization: The Conflict in Theosophy*, 1930, N.V. Theosofische Vereeniging Uitgevers Maatschappij, Available: *http://www.alpheus.org/html/source_materials/krishnamurti/leeuw.html#up*, 13 December 2007.

126   Govert W Schüller, "Krishnamurti and the World Teacher Project: Some Theosophical Perceptions," *Occasional Papers* (Fullerton, CA: Theosophical History, 1997), vol. V, for an excellent examination of the major theories.

127   Annie Besant, "The Boy and the Teacher," *The Star Review* I.1 (1928), 8-9.

128   See Vernon, *Star in the East,* 158-59.

129   Besant, "The Boy and the Teacher," 8-9.

130   George Arundale, who also claimed to channel the Mahatmas at this time, was president of the TS from 1933 until his death in 1945. Vernon, *Star in the East,* 158-59.

131   Jiddu Krishnamurti, "The Purpose of the Order of the Star," *The Star Review* I.12 (Dec. 1928), 423.

132   Annie Besant, *Occultism [Adyar Pamphlet No. 97]*, Jan. 1919, , Available *http://www.theosophical.ca/Occultism AB.htm*, 18 December 2007.

133   Charles Webster Leadbeater, "A Message from the Presiding Bishop," *The Liberal Catholic* X.8 (1930).

134   Krishna had changed the name of the OSE to the Order of the Star in 1928.

135   F.W. Pigott, "Bishop's Notes," *The Liberal Catholic* X.6 (1930).

136   Charles Webster Leadbeater, James I. Wedgwood, Irving Cooper and et al, "The Episcopal Synod and the World Teacher," *The Liberal Catholic* X.7 (1930), 170.

137   F.W. Pigott, "Editorial," *The Liberal Catholic* XV.1 (1934), 3-5.

138   Geoffrey Hodson, *Krishnamurti and the Search for Light*, n.d. [ca. 1939], St. Alban Press, Available: *http://www.alpheus.org/html/source_materials/theosophy/hod son1e.html*, 8 January 2008.

139   F.W. Pigott, 'Bishop's Notes," *The Liberal Catholic* X.7 (1930).

140   Pigott, "Bishop's Notes," i-ii.

141   Francis of Antioch, "Letter," *The Liberal Catholic* XI.1 (Oct. 1931), 28.

142   "Church News," *The Liberal Catholic* XIII.4 (1933).

143   F.W. Pigott, "Bishop's Notes," *The Liberal Catholic* XII.8 (1932).

144   L.J. Bendit, "Letter," *The Liberal Catholic* XIII.4 (1933).

145   F.W. Pigott, "Bishop's Notes," *The Liberal Catholic* XVI.1 (1935).

146   F.W. Pigott, "Bishop's Notes," *The Liberal Catholic* XVI.4 (1936).

147   Maurice Warnon, *C.W. Leadbeater Et J. Krishnamurti*, n.d., The Liberal Catholic Church, Available: *http://kings-garden.org/English/Organizations/LCC.GB/LCIS/Scriptures/Liberal/Leadbeater/@Leadbeater.html*, 23 June 2007.

148   Piepkorn, *Profiles in Belief: The Religious Bodies of the United States and Canada* 296. Anson, *Bishops at Large,* 361.

149   Anson, *Bishops at Large* 363-65. Piepkorn, *Profiles in Belief: The Religious Bodies of the United States and Canada,* 286-309.

150   Email to Siobhán Houston, 29 May 2006.

151   Piepkorn puts his year of birth as 1919, while Tau Mikhael records it as 1916.

152   Newman (b. 1905) was baptized in the Catholic Apostolic (Irvingite) Church. He served as an acolyte in this church for over twenty years. He was ordained to the priesthood in 1938 by James McFall, Regionary Old Catholic Bishop for Ireland. Mathew raised McFall to the episcopate in 1916. Anson, *Bishops at Large* 444-46. Piepkorn, *Profiles in Belief: The Religious Bodies of the United States and Canada* 294-95. Duc de Palatine Richard, *The Pre-Nicene Gnosto-Catholic Church*, 1959, Available: *http://www.gnostic.info/palatine_pre-nicene.html*, 3 January 2008.

153   Piepkorn, *Profiles in Belief: The Religious Bodies of the United States and Canada* 294-95. Anson, *Bishops at Large* 495. Richard, *The Pre-Nicene Gnosto-Catholic Church*. Tau Mikhael, *The Gnostic Tradition in Australia*, n.d., *New Dawn Magazine* (Australia), Available: *http://www.gnostic. info/gnostictradition.html*, 3 January 2008.

154   A.W. Hill, "Exile in Godville: Profile of a Postmodern Heretic," *LA Weekly* 19-25 May 2005. Robert Guffey, *The Suppressed Teachings of Gnosticism: An Interview with Dr. Stephan A. Hoeller*, c. 2003, Available: *http:// www.paranoiamagazine.com/hoeller.html*, 4 January 2008.

155   Guffey, *The Suppressed Teachings of Gnosticism: An Interview with Dr. Stephan A. Hoeller*.

156   William Joseph Whalen, *Separated Brethren: A Survey of Non-Catholic Christian Denominations in the United States* (Milwaukee: Bruce Pub. Co., 1958) 210.

157 Anson, *Bishops at Large* 364. Apostolic Church of Antioch—Malabar Rite web site: http://www.swcp.com/~antioch/

References Cited

Pope Leo VIII. "Humanum Genus". 1884. 2 January 2008. <*http://www.papalencyclicals.net/Leo13/l13human. htm*>.

Ambelain, Robert (Sar Aurifer). "The Martinist Doctrine". n.d. 28 November 2007. <*http://www.ancientmartinistorder. org/Aurifer.htm*>.

Anson, Peter Frederick. *Bishops at Large*. New York: October House, 1965.

Antioch, Francis of. "Letter." *The Liberal Catholic* XI.1 (Oct. 1931): 28.

"Apostolic Succession". San Diego, n.d.: Catholic Answers. 29 March 2006. <*http://www.catholic-forum. com/saints/ncd00687.htm*>.

Ashcraft, W. Michael. *The Dawn of the New Cycle: Point Loma Theosophists and American Culture*. 1st ed. Knoxville: University of Tennessee Press, 2002.

Badertscher, Eric A. "The Measure of a Bishop: The Episcopi Vagantes, Apostolic Succession, and the Legitimacy of the Anglican "Continuing Church" Movement". 1998. Project Canterbury. 4 January 2008. <*http://anglicanhistory.org/essays/badertscher/index.html*>.

Basham, Diana. *The Trial of Woman: Feminism and the Occult Sciences in Victorian Literature and Society*. Houndmills: Macmillan, 1992.

Beckson, Karl E. *London in the 1890s: A Cultural History*. 1st ed. New York: W.W. Norton, 1992.

Bendit, L.J. "Letter." *The Liberal Catholic* XIII.4 (1933): 79.

Besant, Annie. "Occultism [Adyar Pamphlet No. 97]". Jan. 1919. *The Theosophist Vol. XXXV*. . 18 December 2007. <*http://www.theosophical.ca/OccultismAB.htm*>.

—-. "The Boy and the Teacher." *The Star Review* I.1 (1928): 8-9.

Blaufuss, Dietrich. "Pietism." *Dictionary of Gnosis and Western Esotericism*. Ed. Wouter J. Hanegraaff. Vol. 2. Leiden: Brill, 2005. 956-60.

Bown, Nicola, Carolyn Burdett, and Pamela Thurschwell. *The Victorian Supernatural*. Cambridge Studies in Nineteenth-Century Literature and Culture; 42. Cambridge: Cambridge University Press, 2004.

Bozoky, Edina. "Catharism." *Dictionary of Gnosis and Western Esotericism*. Ed. Wouter J. Hanegraaff. Vol. 1. Leiden: Brill, 2005. 242-47.

Brandreth, Henry *Episcopi Vagantes and the Anglican Church*. London: Society for Promoting Christian Knowledge, 1947.

Bricaud, Bishop Jean (Tau Jean II). "Patriarchal Homily". 1908. Trans. by Phillip A. Garver. 21 December 2007. <*http://www.gnostique.net/documents/homeliej2.htm*>.

Bricaud, Joanny. "Profession De Foi". n.d. 12 December 2007. <*http://user.cyberlink.ch/~koenig/profess.htm*>.

Briggs, Robin. *Communities of Belief: Cultural and Social Tension in Early Modern France*. Oxford: Oxford University Press, 1989.

Brooke, John Hedley. *Science and Religion: Some Historical Perspectives*. Cambridge History of Science. Cambridge: Cambridge University Press, 1991.

Burton, Dan, and David Grandy. *Magic, Mystery, and Science: The Occult in Western Civilization*. Bloomington: Indiana University Press, 2004.

Burton, Richard D. E. *Blood in the City: Violence and Revelation in Paris, 1789-1954*. Ithaca: Cornell University Press, 2001.

Butler, Alison. "Magical Beginnings: The Intellectual Origins of the Victorian Occult Revival." *Limina: A Journal of Historical and Cultural Studies* 9 (2003): 78-95.

Caillet, Serge. "Martinism Today". 2000. 30 December 2007. <*http://www.france-spiritualites.fr/interview-serge-caillet-martinism-today.htm*>.

Campbell, Bruce F. *Ancient Wisdom Revised: A History of the Theosophical Movement*. Berkeley: University of California Press, 1980.

Campbell, Peter Robert. *Power and Politics in Old Regime France, 1720-1745*. London: Routledge, 1996.

Canada, Christian Catholic Church. "Most Reverend J. René Vilatte (1854-1929)". Gatineau, Québec, n.d.: Biography of Vilatte. Christian Catholic Church Canada. 28 December 2007. <*http://ccrcc.ca/en/episcopal_committee/cccc/mem_jr_vilatte.html* >.

"Catholic Encyclopedia, Apocatastasis". 1913. 8 January 2008. <*http://www.newadvent.org/cathen/01599a.htm*>.

"Catholic Encyclopedia, Archdiocese of Utrecht". 1913. 1 January 2008 2007. <*http://www.newadvent.org/cathen/15245a.htm*>.

"Catholic Encyclopedia, Arnauld". 1913. 4 January 2008. <*http://www.newadvent.org/cathen/01742a.htm*>.

"Catholic Encyclopedia, Jansenius and Jansenism". 1913. 3 January 2008. <*http://www.newadvent.org/cathen/08285a.htm*>.

"Catholic Encyclopedia, Port-Royal". 1913. 3 January 2008. <*http://www.newadvent.org/cathen/12295a.htm*>.

"Catholic Encyclopedia, Schism". 1913. 2 January 2008. <*http://www.newadvent.org/cathen/13529a.htm*>.

"Catholic Encyclopedia, the French Concordat of 1801". 1913. 6 January 2008. <*http://www.newadvent.org/cathen/04204a.htm*>.

Cekada, Rev. Anthony, SSPX. "A Warning on the Old Catholics: False Bishops, False Churches". 1980. *The Roman Catholic*. 12 December 2007. <*http://sspx.agenda.tripod.com/id73.html*>.

Chadwick, Owen. *The Spirit of the Oxford Movement: Tractarian Essays*. Cambridge: Cambridge University Press, 1990.

"Church News." *The Liberal Catholic* XIII.4 (1933): 63-64.

Church, Old Catholic. "A Short History". n.d.: Old Catholic Church of America. 4 January 2008. <*http://www.oldcatholic.org/history.htm*>.

Davidoff, Lenore. "Class and Gender in Victorian England." *Sex and Class in Women's History*. Eds. Judith Lowder Newton, Mary P. Ryan and Judith R. Walkowitz. London: Routledge and Kegan Paul, 1983.

Devlin, Judith. *The Superstitious Mind: French Peasants and the Supernatural in the Nineteenth Century*. New Haven: Yale University Press, 1987.

Dixon, Joy. *Divine Feminine: Theosophy and Feminism in England*. Baltimore: Johns Hopkins University Press, 2001.

Doinel, Jules Stany. "Le Rituel De L'appareillamentum". n.d. 12 December 2007. <*http://user.cyberlink.ch/ ~koenig/appareil.htm*>.

——. "Rituel De La Fraction Du Pain". n.d. 8 August 2007. <*http://user.cyberlink.ch/~koenig/pain.htm*>.

——. "The First Homily: "On the Holy Gnosis"". 1890. 21 December 2007. <*http://www.gnostique.net/documents/ homelie1.htm*>.

——. "The Valentinian Gnosis". 31 December 2007. <*http://www.gnostique.net/documents/ValGnose.htm*>.

Doyle, William. *Jansenism: Catholic Resistance to Authority from the Reformation to the French Revolution*. Studies in European History. Basingstoke: Macmillan, 2000.

——. *The Old European Order, 1660-1800*. Oxford: Oxford University Press, 1992.

Encausse, Philippe. *Papus, Le Balzac De L'occultisme: Vingt-Cinq Annees D'occultisme Occidental*. Paris: Pierre Belfond, 1979.

Erb, Peter C. *Pietists: Selected Writings*. New York: Paulist Press, 1983.

Faivre, Antoine. *Access to Western Esotericism*. Albany: State University of New York Press, 1994.

——. "The Notions of Concealment and Secrecy in Modern Esoteric Currents since the Renaissance (a Methodological Approach)." *Rending the Veil: Concealment and Secrecy in the History of Religions*. Ed. Elliot R. Wolfson. New York: Seven Bridges Press, 1999.

Faught, C. Brad. *The Oxford Movement: A Thematic History of the Tractarians and Their Times*. University Park, PA: Pennsylvania State University Press, 2003.

Ferguson, Thomas. "The Enthralling Power: History and Heresy in John Henry Newman." *Anglican Theological Review* (2003).

Feuerhahn, Ronald R. "The Roots and Fruits of Pietism". St. Louis, MO, 1998. *Pieper Lectures* Concordia Historical Institute and the Luther Academy. 31 December 2007. <*http://www.mtio.com/articles/aissar3.htm*>.

Fyfe, Aileen, and John van Whye. "Victorian Science and Religion". n.d. *The Victorian Web*. 12 December 2007. <*http://www.victorianweb.org/science/science&religion.html*>.

Gardner, E.L. "There Is No Religion Higher Than Truth: Developments in the Theosophical Society". London, 1963. The Theosophical Publishing House, Ltd. 24 December 2007. <*http://www.theosophical.ca/NoReligion .htm*>.

Garver, Phillip A. "The History of the Gnostic Church". 2001-2006. 3 January 2008 <*http://www.plerome.org/his- toire.htm*>.

Geyraud, Pierre. "Gnostic Priestess," Translated by Phillip A. Garver, from *Les Petites Églises De Paris* (Parmi Les Sects Et Les Rites). Paris: Editions Emile-Paul Frères) 76-83.

1937. 5 January 2008. <*http://www.gnostique.net/documents/pretresse.htm*>.

Gilbert, R.A. *A.E. Waite: Magician of Many Parts*. Kent, UK: Aquarian Press, 1987.

"Gnostics Still a Church: With 250 Members in the World—Head in France a Bookkeeper." *New York Times* 27 November 1910.

Godwin, Joscelyn. "Lady Caithness and Her Connection with Theosophy." *Theosophical History* VIII.4 (2000): 127-47.

—-. *The Beginnings of Theosophy in France*. London: Theosophical History Centre, 1989.

—-. *The Theosophical Enlightenment*. Albany: State University of New York Press, 1994.

Goodrick-Clarke, Nicholas. "Hermeticism and Hermetic Societies." *Dictionary of Gnosis and Western Esotericism*. Ed. Wouter J. Hanegraaff. Vol. 1. Leiden: Brill, 2005. 550-58.

Grafton, Charles Chapman. *The Lineage of the American Catholic Church, Commonly Called the Episcopal Church*. Milwaukee, WI: The Young Churchman Company, 1911.

Grafton, Charles Chapman *A Journey Godward of [a Servant of Jesus Christ]* Milwaukee: Young Churchman Co., 1910.

Guenin-Lelle, Dianne. "Friends' Theological Heritage: From Seventeenth-Century Quietists to a Guide to True

Peace". 2002. *Quaker Theology*. 31 December 2008. <*http://www.quaker.org/quest/iss_e6-contents.html*>.

Guffey, Robert. "The Suppressed Teachings of Gnosticism: An Interview with Dr. Stephan A. Hoeller". c. 2003. *Paranoia Vol. 34*. 4 January 2008. <*http://www.paranoia-magazine.com/hoeller.html*>.

Hanegraaff, Wouter J. *New Age Religion and Western Culture : Esotericism in the Mirror of Secular Thought.* Albany: State University of New York, 1998.

Hill, A.W. "Exile in Godville Profile of a Postmodern Heretic." *LA Weekly* 19-25 May 2005, *www.gnosis.org/LAWeekly.htm* ed.

Hodson, Geoffrey. "Introduction". n.p., n.d. [c. 1965]. *C.W. Leadbeater: A Great Occultist.* Eds. Sandra Hodson and Matthias J. van Thiel. 4 January 2008. <*http://www.alpheus.org/html/articles/theosophy/oncwl1.html#t1*>.

—. "Krishnamurti and the Search for Light". Sydney, n.d. [ca. 1939]. St. Alban Press. 8 January 2008. <*http://www.alpheus.org/html/source_materials/theosophy/hodson1e.html*>.

Hogue, William M. "The Episcopal Church and Archbishop Vilatte." *Historical Magazine of the Protestant Episcopal Church* XXXIV.1 (1955), 35-55.

Hussey, J.M. *The Orthodox Church in the Byzantine Empire.* Oxford: Clarendon, 1990.

Introvigne, Massimo. "Martinism: Second Period." *Dictionary of Gnosis and Western Esotericism*. Ed. Wouter J. Hanegraaff. Vol. 2. Leiden: Brill, 2005. 780-83.

---. "Neo-Catharism." *Dictionary of Gnosis and Western Esotericism*. Ed. Wouter J. Hanegraaff. Vol. 2. Leiden: Brill, 2005. 826-28.

Israel, Jonathan. *The Dutch Republic: Its Rise, Greatness, and Fall, 1477-1806.* . Oxford: Clarendon Press, 1995.

Kemp, Leah. "Shepherd or Wolf? Joseph René Vilatte in Francophone Wisconsin." Green Bay, WI, 2001. University of Wisconsin. 15 December 2007. <*http://www.uwgb.edu/wisfrench/study/old_catholics/old_cath olics.htm*>.

Kolakowski, Leslek. "Quietism." *Encyclopedia of Religion*. Ed. Lindsay Jones. 2nd ed. Detroit: Macmillan Reference USA, 2005. 7557-59.

Krishnamurti, Jiddu. "The Purpose of the Order of the Star." *The Star Review* I.12 (Dec. 1928): 423.

Kwasniewski, Peter A. "The Conversion of John Henry Newman". 1999. *Faith*. 13 December 2007. <*http://www.catholic.net/rcc/Periodicals/Faith/JAN-FEB99/Conversion.html*>.

Lambert, Malcolm. *The Cathars*. Oxford: Blackwell, 1998.

Laurant, Jean-Pierre. *L'esoterisme Chrétien En France Au Xixe Siecle*. Lausanne: L'Age d'homme, 1992.

—-. "The Primitive Characteristics of Nineteenth-Century Esotericism." *Modern Esoteric Spirituality*. Eds. Antoine Faivre and Jacob Needleman. London: SCM Press Ltd, 1993.

Le Forestier, Rene. *L'occultisme En France Aux Xixeme Et Xxeme Siecles: L'église Gnostique*. Ed. Antoine Faivre. Milano: Arche, 1990.

Le Forestier, Rene, Antoine Faivre, and Alec Mellor. *La Franc-Maconnerie Templiere Et Occultiste Aux Xviiie Et Xixe Siecles*. Paris: La Table d'emeraude, 1987.

Leadbeater, Charles Webster. "A Message from the Presiding Bishop.' *The Liberal Catholic* X.8 (1930): 200-08.

—-. "Hidden Side of Christian Festivals." *The Liberal Catholic* II.1 (1925).

—-. "The Masters and the Path". 1940 (1st ed. 1925). Anand Golap. 1 December 2007. <*http://www.anandgholap.net/Masters_And_Path-CWL.htm*>.

—-. *The Science of the Sacraments*. Eleventh reprint ed. Adyar: Theosophical Publishing House, 1999.

Leadbeater, Charles Webster, James I. Wedgwood, and Annie Besant. *Occultism of the Mass and the Old Catholic Church Movement. A Collection of Essays from Writings and Documents*. Krotona. Theosophical Publishing House, 1918.

Leadbeater, Charles Webster, et al. "The Episcopal Synod and the World Teacher." *The Liberal Catholic* X.7 (1930): 170.

Lenardon, Joan. "The Civil Constitution of the Clergy as Seen by the Journal Encyclopédique". Toronto, 1972. *Historical Studies (Canadian Catholic Historical Association)*. Canadian Catholic Historical Association. 4 January 2008. <*http://www.umanitoba.ca/colleges/st_pauls/ccha/Back%20Issues/CCHA1972/Lenardon.html*>.

Levine, Philippa. *Feminist Lives in Victorian England: Private Roles and Public Commitment*. Oxford: B. Blackwell, 1990.

Magraw, Roger. *France, 1800-1914 : A Social History*. London ; New York: Longman, 2002.

Mathew, Arnold Harris. *An Episcopal Odyssey. An Open Letter to the Archbishop of Canterbury, Etc.*: Kingsdown, 1915.

Mazet, Edward. "Freemasonry and Esotericism." *Modern Esoteric Spirituality*. Eds. Antoine Faivre and Jacob Needleman. London: SCM Press Ltd, 1993.

McCalla, Arthur. "Louis-Claude De Saint-Martin." *Dictionary of Gnosis and Western Esotericism*. Ed. Wouter J. Hanegraaff. Vol. 2, 2005. 1024-31.

McIntosh, Christopher. *Eliphas Lévi and the French Occult Revival*. London: Rider and Company, 1972.

McManners, John. *Church and Society in Eighteenth-Century France*. Vol. 2. 2 vols Oxford: Clarendon Press, 1998.

—-. *The Oxford Illustrated History of Christianity*. Oxford: Oxford University Press, 1990.

Meyer, Anna. *Hunting the Double Helix: How DNA Is Solving Puzzles of the Past*. Crows Nest, NSW, Australia: Allen & Unwin, 2005.

Meyer, Marvin, and James M. Robinson. *The Nag Hammadi Scriptures*. San Francisco: HarperOne, 2007.

Moorman, John R. H. . *A History of the Church in England*. New York: Morehouse-Gorham, 1954.

Morse, David. *High Victorian Culture*. Houndmills: Macmillan, 1993.

Moss, Claude Beaufort. *The Old Catholic Movement, Its Origins and History...Second Edition*. London: S.P.C.K, 1964.

Noakes, Richard. "Spiritualism, Science and the Supernatural in Mid-Victorian Britain." *The Victorian Supernatural*. Eds. Nicola Bown, Carolyn Burdett and Pamela Thurschwell. Cambridge Studies in Nineteenth-Century Literature and Culture: 42. Cambridge, UK: Cambridge University Press, 2004. 23-43.

Oppenheim, Janet. *The Other World: Spiritualism and Psychical Research in England, 1850-1914*. Cambridge: Cambridge University Press, 1985.

Owen, Alex. *The Darkened Room: Women, Power and Spiritualism in Late Victorian England*. Philadelphia: University of Pennsylvania Press, 1990.

—-. *The Place of Enchantment: British Occultism and the Culture of the Modern*. Chicago: University of Chicago Press, 2004.

Pagels, Elaine. *The Gnostic Gospels*. New York: Random House, 1981.

Parmentier, Martien. "Water Baptism and Spirit Baptism in the Church Fathers". 1998. *Cyberjournal for Pentecostal-Charismatic Research*. 2 January 2008. <*http://www.pctii.org/cyberj/cyber3.html*>.

Parry, D. L. L., and Pierre Girard. *France since 1800: Squaring the Hexagon*. Oxford: Oxford University Press, 2002.

Partridge, Christopher H. *The Re-Enchantment of the West: Alternative Spiritualities, Sacralization, Popular Culture, and Occulture*. 2 vols. London: T & T Clark International, 2004.

Perkin, Joan. *Victorian Women*. London: J. Murray, 1993.

Pert, Alan. *Red Cactus: The Life of Anna Kingsford*. 2nd. ed. NSW, Australia: Books and Writers 2007.

Pickering, W. S. F. *Anglo-Catholicism: A Study in Religious Ambiguity*. London: Routledge, 1989.

Piepkorn, Arthur Carl. *Profiles in Belief: The Religious Bodies of the United States and Canada.* New York: Harper & Row, 1977.

Pigott, F.W. "Bishop's Notes." *The Liberal Catholic* XVI.4 (1936).

—. "Bishop's Notes." *The Liberal Catholic* XII.8 (1932).

—. "Bishop's Notes." *The Liberal Catholic* XVI.1 (1935).

—. "Bishop's Notes." *The Liberal Catholic* X.9 (1930).

—. "Bishop's Notes." *The Liberal Catholic* X.7 (1930).

—. "Editorial." *The Liberal Catholic* XV.1 (1934): 3-5.

Pigott, F.W. "Bishop's Notes.' *The Liberal Catholic* X.6 (1930).

Platt, Warren Christopher. "The Liberal Catholic Church: An Analysis of a Hybrid Sect " Dissertation. Columbia University 1982.

Plummer, John P. *The Many Paths of the Independent Sacramental Movement.* Dallas: Newt Books, 2005.

Prescott, Andrew. "'Builders of the Temple of the New Civilisation': Annie Besant and Freemasonry". Sheffield, n.d.: 1-9. University of Sheffield Centre for Research into Freemasonry. 1 December 2007. *<http://freemasonry.dept. shef.ac.uk/pdf/besant.pdf >.*

Pruter, Karl, and J. Gordon Melton. *The Old Catholic Sourcebook.* New York: Garland, 1983.

Richard, Duc de Palatine. "The Pre-Nicene Gnosto-Catholic Church". 1959. *Lucis Magazine.* New Dawn Magazine (Australia) 3 January 2008. <*http://www.gnostic. info/palatine_pre-nicene.html*>.

Rowell, Geoffrey. *The Vision Glorious: Themes and Personalities of the Catholic Revival in Anglicanism.* Oxford: Oxford University Press, 1983.

Rudorff, Raymond. *The Belle Epoque.* New York: Saturday Review Press, 1973.

Ryan, Charles J. *H. P. Blavatsky and the Theosophical Movement.* Pasadena, CA: Theosophical University Press, 1975.

Santucci, James A. "Theosophical Society." *Dictionary of Gnosis and Western Esotericism.* Ed. Wouter J. Hanegraaff. Vol. 2. Leiden: Brill, 2005. 1114-23.

Schaff, Phillip. *Creeds of Christendom, with a History and Critical Notes (Sixth Edition).* 1877. Vol. 1. 3 vols, 1919.

Schama, Simon. *The Embarrassment of Riches: An Interpretation of Dutch Culture in the Golden Age.* New York: Knopf, 1987.

Schlossberg, Herbert. "Religious Revival and the Transformation of English Sensibilities in the Early Nineteeenth Century". Provincetown, RI, n.d.: Prof. George Landow, Brown University. 11 December 2007. <*http://www.victorianweb.org/religion/intro.html*>.

Schuler, Christoph. *The Mathew Affair: The Failure to Establish an Old Catholic Church in England in the Context of Anglican Old Catholic Relations between 1902 and 1925* Amersfoot: Stichting Centraal Oud-Katholiek Boekhuis, 1997.

Schüller, Govert W. "Krishnamurti and the World Teacher Project: Some Theosophical Perceptions." *Occasional Papers*. Fullerton, CA: Theosophical History, 1997. Vol. V.

Smoley, Richard. *Forbidden Faith: The Gnostic Legacy from the Gospels to the Da Vinci Code*. San Francisco: HarperSanFrancisco, 2006.

—. *Inner Christianity : A Guide to the Esoteric Tradition*. Boston: Shambhala, 2002.

Steiner, Rudolf. *The Spiritual Guidance of the Individual and Humanity*. Trans. Samuel Desch. Hudson, NY: Anthroposophic Press, 1991.

Synesius. *L'arbre Gnostique*. Paris: Chamuel, 1899.

Tarnas, Richard. *The Passion of the Western Mind*. New York: Ballantine Books, 1991.

Tau Mikhael. "The Gnostic Tradition in Australia". n.d.: New Dawn Magazine (Australia). 3 January 2008. <http://www.gnostic.info/gnostictradition.html>.

Taylor, Anne. *Annie Besant : A Biography*. Oxford: Oxford University Press, 1992.

Thériault, Msgr. Serge A. "Gaston J. Fercken, 1855-1930". 16 February 2007. <*http://www.ccrcc.ca/documents/gjfercken.pdf*>.

Theriault, Serge A. *Msgr. Rene Vilatte: Community Organizer of Religion, 1854-1929*. 1997. 2nd ed. Berkeley: Apocryphile Press, 2006.

Thompson, Micheal [sic]. "More Catholic Than the Pope? Varieties of 'Schism' in the Catholic Church in France, 1800-2000." *Comparative Culture: The Journal of Miyazaki International College* 10 (2004).

Tillett, Gregory. *The Elder Brother*. London: Routledge & Kegan Paul Books, Ltd., 1982.

Tingay, Kevin. "The Ritual Dimension of Theosophy: Some Forgotten Endeavours." *Theosophical History* X.3 (July 2004): 7-15.

Tombs, Robert. *France 1814-1914*. London: Longman, 1996.

Toth, Ladislaus. "Gnostic Church." *Dictionary of Gnosis and Western Esotericism*. Ed. Wouter J. Hanegraaff. Vol. I. Leiden: Brill, 2001. 400-03.

Turner, Frank M. *Contesting Cultural Authority: Essays in Victorian Intellectual Life*. Cambridge: Cambridge University Press, 1993.

van der Leeuw, Johannes Jacobus. "Revelation or Realization: The Conflict in Theosophy". Amsterdam, 1930. N.V. Theosofische Vereeniging Uitgevers

Maatschappij. 13 December 2007. <*http://www.alpheus. org/html/source_materials/krishnamurti/leeuw.html#up*>.

van Kley, Dale. *The Jansenists and the Expulsion of the Jesuits from France, 1757-1765*. New Haven: Yale University Press, 1975.

Var, Jean-Francois. "Martines De Pasqually." *Dictionary of Gnosis and Western Esotericism*. Ed. Wouter J. Hanegraaff. Vol. 2. Leiden: Brill, 2005. 931-36.

Vernon, Roland. *Star in the East*. Boulder, CO: Sentient Publications, 2002.

Versluis, Arthur. "Christian Theosophical Literature of the Seventeenth and Eighteenth Centuries." *Gnosis and Hermeticism: From Antiquity to Modern Times*. Eds. Roelef van der Broek and Wouter J. Hanegraaff. Albany: State University Press of New York, 1998.

Vignot, Bernard. *Les Églises Parallèles*. Paris: Cerf, 1991.

Vilatte, Joseph Rene. *Chivalrous & Religious Order of the Crown of Thorns Statutes*. Fort Howard, WI: James Kerr & Son, 1893.

Waite, Arthur Edward. *Devil Worship in France or the Question of Lucifer*. London: George Redway, 1896.

—-. *The Unknown Philosopher: The Life of Louis Claude De St.Martin and the Substance of His Transcendental Doctrine*. Montana, USA: Kessinger Publishing Company, n.d.

Wallace, Peter George. *The Long European Reformation: Religion, Political Conflict, and the Search for Conformity, 1350-1750*. New York: Palgrave Macmillan, 2003.

Walsh, Walter. *The Secret History of the Oxford Movement*. London: Swan Sonnenschein, 1897.

Warnon, Maurice. "Biography [of James Ingall Wedgwood]". n.d.: Liberal Catholic Church. 4 January 2008. <*http://kingsgarden.org/English/Organizations/LCC.gb/LCIS/Scriptures/Liberal/Wedgwood/WedgwoodBiography.html*>.

—. "C.W. Leadbeater Et J. Krishnamurti". n.d.: The Liberal Catholic Church. 23 June 2007. <*http://kingsgarden.org/English/Organizations/LCC.GB/LCIS/Scriptures/Liberal/Leadbeater/@Leadbeater.html* >.

Wasserstrom, Steven M. *Religion after Religion : Gershom Scholem, Mircea Eliade, and Henry Corbin at Eranos*. Princeton, N.J.: Princeton University Press, 1999.

Wedgwood, James I. "The Beginnings of the Liberal Catholic Church". 1937. *UBIQUE Magazine*. Global Library. 12 December 2007. <*http://www.global.org/Pub/JIW_History.asp*>.

—. *The Presence of Christ in the Holy Communion and Other Writings*. London: St Alban's Press, 1984.

Weeks, Donald Pierce. "Joseph Rene Vilatte: First Independent Catholic Prelate in North America". n.d. 31 December 2007. <*http://www.concentric.net/~Cosmas/vilatte.htm*>.

Whalen, William Joseph. *Separated Brethren: A Survey of Non-Catholic Christian Denominations in the United States.* Milwaukee: Bruce Pub. Co., 1953.

Wilson, Colin. *The Occult.* New York: Random House, 1971.

Yates, Frances Amelia. *The Rosicrucian Enlightenment.* Boston: Shambhala, 1978.